FROM THE AUTHOR OF
Beyond Basketballs

Books

Strategic Marketing For The Digital Age
Grow Your Business With Online and Digital Technology

Global Marketing For The Digital Age
How To Expand Your Business in The Global Marketplace
Using Advanced Digital Technology

How To Sell A Lobster
The Money-Making Secrets of A Streetwise Entrepreneur

The Problem With Penguins
Stand Out In A Crowded Marketplace By Packaging Your BIG IDEA

Educational CD/Booklets

Packaging The Invisible Box

How To Create A Marketing Plan That Works

The 25 Packaging Mistakes and How To Avoid Them

The 13 BIG Idea Strategies

The Last Goal

The Transformation Economy

The Publishing Success Solution

Visit www.BishopBigIdeas.com
for all of Bill's latest creations

BEYOND BASKETBALLS

THE NEW REVOLUTIONARY WAY TO BUILD A SUCCESSFUL BUSINESS IN TODAY'S POST-PRODUCT WORLD

BILL BISHOP

iUniverse, Inc.
Bloomington

Beyond Basketballs
The New Revolutionary Way To Build A Successful
Business In A Post-Product World

Copyright © 2010 Bill Bishop

All rights reserved. No part of this book may be used or reproduced by any means, graphic, electronic, or mechanical, including photocopying, recording, taping or by any information storage retrieval system without the written permission of the publisher except in the case of brief quotations embodied in critical articles and reviews.

iUniverse books may be ordered through booksellers or by contacting:

iUniverse
1663 Liberty Drive
Bloomington, IN 47403
www.iuniverse.com
1-800-Authors (1-800-288-4677)

Because of the dynamic nature of the Internet, any Web addresses or links contained in this book may have changed since publication and may no longer be valid. The views expressed in this work are solely those of the author and do not necessarily reflect the views of the publisher, and the publisher hereby disclaims any responsibility for them.

ISBN: 978-1-4502-6632-1 (pbk)
ISBN: 978-1-4502-1203-8 (ebk)

Printed in the United States of America

iUniverse rev. date: 12/17/2010

Praise for Bill's book *How To Sell A Lobster*

My husband and I really enjoyed your book. So much excellent advice in such a complete package! We are impressed! But we must know: "Who is Marketing Mike? Please reveal the mystery! Thanks for improving our business!
Jamie and Kelly

My name is Taseo. I am a third year BBA student. I have just finished reading your book *How To Sell A Lobster* and I can honestly say I learned more about marketing than in my recent 5 month marketing course. The material was simple to digest which was a real treat for me since it is a big change from overly wordy and flat out boring marketing text books. I just wanted to thank you for writing this book and allowing me to share the experience you've gained in the marketing world.
Taseo

I have just finished reading your book *How To Sell A Lobster*. It was fascinating and I couldn't put it down until I had finished reading it cover to cover. Most of the challenges that were described in your book are exactly the challenges that we are facing as a small company trying to "get off the ground". I am very interested in exploring in more detail how those marketing strategies could be applied to our business.
Pat

Hi, my name is Natalie and I am 12 years old. I read the book *How to Sell A Lobster* and I enjoyed it very much and finished it in only three days! My favorite story was The Line-Up, because I found it was a very smart way to make customers interested in your business. My mom and I enjoyed your book and we thought it was very funny. My mom thinks that Marketing Mike is you and I am not quite sure. If you could please reply and let us know who Marketing Mike is we would really appreciate it. Thank you.
Natalie

Really enjoyed your book. I am applying some of your ideas to my business. I'll bite, who is Marketing Mike?
Mike

Found that your book *How To Sell A Lobster* was spell binding and I was unable to put it down. So I did not until I finished. One question though: Who is Marketing Mike? We will be trying The Three Boxes in our business presentation. Thank You.
Brian & Diana

I have read your book many times since I received it. There is so much information that I can use in my business. Thanks very much for a great book. Now to the question! Who is Marketing Mike? I am very curious. Thanks.
Betty

I just finished your book *How To Sell A Lobster*. It is an absolutely fantastic book! I thoroughly enjoyed every single chapter - each one packed with valuable information, and written in an extremely easy to read writing style! This is definitely one of the most "valuable" books I have read, and I have read a LOT of books over the years! I will definitely be APPLYING it!
Wayne

I have just completed reading your book *How To Sell A Lobster* for the first time. I will guarantee there will be many rereads. It was an extremely interesting and eye-opening experience. I am also glad to learn that you are Canadian. I think it is well overdo that we have some Canadian talent of this quality.
Chris

I gave *How To Sell A Lobster* to my brother-in-law who owns a small bakery. At first he told me he would never read it (he's not a "reader"). I gave it to him anyway. He started reading it and then called me up and couldn't stop raving about how good the book was (gee . . . what a surprise!). He then wanted to find out where he could get more of these books. He wanted to give one to his manager and a few more copies for his business partners. He feels every business owner should read *How To Sell A Lobster*!
Pat

I just read your book *How To Sell A Lobster*, and as a partner in a small consulting firm, I found it enjoyable and insightful. I have also asked my colleagues to read it. I am hopeful that we can apply some of the learning, as we relate to so many of the examples described. I wanted to take a minute and thank you for sharing the experience.
Khan

Well, Mr. Bishop you've peaked my curiosity. I have just finished *How To Sell A Lobster* and must know, who is Marketing Mike? Besides having a wealth of knowledge and insight into human nature, he must also be one of great generosity to have shared his wisdom so willingly with you. My curiosity is peaked….please tell me who is Marketing Mike?
Poseann

I am reading your book for a second time. Your teaching and techniques are an eye opener and have really stuck with me. At the first time of reading I didn't implement anything so upon reading your book the second time, I put your techniques to work at a yard sale I did and it was amazing how much I sold by giving people a choice, i.e. 1 item for $1 or any 2 for $1.50. I worked with myself to look at what I was doing as marketing items I no longer needed and someone else did. I am looking forward to utilizing your teaching in other areas of my life and helping my grown children as well.
Irene

Where were you three years ago? I have been struggling to keep my head above water in this business (which I love very much) but it's tough. The "Lobster" book was excellent.
Lucio

I just finished reading your book *How To Sell A Lobster*. Great read! And I must say, I love the ideas and mind set you create. I am fascinated by many of the principles your book *How To Sell A Lobster* defines/shares. And as an actor, I am trying to apply these principles to what I do and my career.
David

I read your book and loved it. Every word, every page...
Shelly

My name is Olga. I am from Ufa, the big city in the middle of Russia. I decided to write this letter with words of gratitude for your book *How To Sell A Lobster*. When I took this small book in my hands in a bookshop firstly I was not impressed much but I decided to buy it. I was very surprised. I found all advice from the book very useful for my retail business. Especially I was impressed with an advice "Three Boxes". Now, when a customer is in my coffee-tea boutique, my seller asks him: "How much of product do you want to buy: 100, 150 or 200 grams?" And 8 from 10 customers usually answer "150", and sometimes "200"! Although the minimum volume of purchase is 50 grams. Other advice also useful. For example, the advice about "box of chocolate". We made mini-pockets with tea (just for a one cup) and now offer them to vacillating customers with floor prices. And often these people come back to our boutique to buy bigger volume of tea. So I would like to tell thank you very much for your book *How To Sell A Lobster*.
Olga

I read your book (the Romanian translation) in couple of hours after my wife bought it. I was happy and nervous in the same time. Happy because I saw in Marketing Mike someone that I have been for most of my friends and most of my employers (if they were smart enough to listen), and nervous to see that I did not consider doing from this as a business.
Razvan

I wanted to take this opportunity to congratulate you on your success. Amongst all the glitter and clutter of business books in the market, it's comforting to find a message that speaks clearly to small businesses and delivers real applicable concepts that are adaptable to the entrepreneurs of the world. I recently ordered 5 copies of your book, *How To Sell A Lobster*, through Amazon.ca. I feel it's the perfect gift for some of my small business clients who struggle to grasp some of the key marketing concepts that could propel their endeavors to the next level of success. Your presentation methods are classic, simple and most of all direct,

enabling you to reach your audience on a deeper level. I've read through my copy six or seven times and keep coming back for reminders. Keep up the good work and I look forward to your upcoming releases.
Joey

To order *How To Sell A Lobster*, visit **BishopBigIdeas.com** or call 416.364.8770.

To Douglas & Robin

I am sure you will go well
beyond basketballs in the 21st Century

Contents

Introduction: Building the Better Boat — xix

Chapter 1: The Relationship-First Formula — 1

Trinity Gear & Rod: Trying to succeed in today's world — 2
The Relationship-First Formula — 8
Syntax Switching: Caught in the Product-First Trap — 9
The Basketball People: A Relationship-First Enterprise — 10
A Tale of Two Formulas — 13
My Moment of Enlightenment — 14

Chapter 2: The Post-Product Reality — 16

Reality #1: The rate of change is accelerating — 17
Reality #2: Commodity margins are collapsing — 19
Reality #3: Consumers rule the marketplace — 21
Reality #4: Prospects are harder to reach — 24
Reality #5. Markets and channels are fragmented — 27
Reality #6. Product life cycles are shrinking — 29
Reality #7: Technology plays a pivotal role — 32
Reality #8: Existing markets are not enough — 35
Facing Up To The Post-Product Reality — 36

Chapter 3: The Performance Plateau — 37

The Performance Plateau — 38
Limiting Factor #1: Focusing on short-term goals — 38
Limiting Factor #2: Working as individuals or small groups — 39
Limiting Factor #3: Thinking only about products and services — 40
Limiting Factor #4: Trying to beat the competition — 41
Limiting Factor #5: Focus on sales, not marketing — 42
Limiting Factor #6: Creating tools for specific situations — 43
Limiting Factor #7: Being a slave of technology — 44
Limiting Factor #8: Focusing only on existing markets — 45

Chapter 4: The Principal Strategies — 47

Principal Strategy #1: Start with a Customer Type — 48
Principal Strategy #2: Don't Compete; Provide Unique Value — 52
Principal Strategy #3. Deliver Unique Value Through Teamwork — 55
Principal Strategy #4: Envision Ideal System Models — 61
Principal Strategy #5: Give Away Value to Start Quality Relationships — 65
Principal Strategy #6: Offer Components of Unique Value — 68
Principal Strategy #7: Develop a Mass Customization Planning Process — 71
Principal Strategy #8: Develop Capabilities, not Tools — 74
Principal Strategy #9: Ride The Strategic Dip — 79

Chapter 5: The Relationship-First Enterprise — 82

Business Model Based On the Relationship-First Formula — 83
Strategy Starts With Customer Type — 83
Unique Value Divided Into Components — 84
Capabilities Developed to Assemble Value Components — 84
Free Value Given to Start Relationships — 85
Marketing Program Created Around Customer Type — 86
Quality Relationships Fostered Using Centralized Database System — 87
Communicate on Mass, Individualized Basis — 87
Organizational Structure Based on the Relationship-First Formula — 89
Strategic Planning and System Process Ensures Progress — 91
Putting the Relationship-First Model into Action — 92

Chapter 6: Relationship-First Enterprise Scenarios — 93

Scenario #1: The Excelsior Drug Company — 93
Scenario #2: The Pecunia Financial Corporation — 95
Scenario #3: The Tiger Lilly Tea Co. — 98
Scenario #4: The Golf Course Manager Co. — 100
Scenario #5: Icarus Airlines — 102
Scenario #6: VIXVAC Heating & Air-Conditioning — 104
Making the Transformation — 107

Chapter 7: The Transformation 108
    Step #1: Create Your Relationship-First Team 109
    Step #2: Choose Your Customer Type 111
    Step #3: List Your Value Components 113
    Step #4: Develop Your Controlling Promotional Idea 116
    Step #5: Determine The Free Value To Give Away 118
    Step #6: Craft A Unified Message 119
    Step #7: Establish Your Graphic Identity 120
    Step #8: Build Your People Database 121
    Step #9: Integrate Your Information Systems 122
    Step #10: Develop Interactive Communications Tools ... 125
    Step #11: Launch Your Controlling Promotional Idea ... 126
    Step #12: Foster Long-Term, Quality Relationships 129

Epilogue 131

Glossary 135

Acknowledgements 139

Preface To New Edition

It's been more than ten years since the first edition of this book was published under the title of The Strategic Enterprise. Since then, so much has happened. 9/11. Two wars. The election of Barack Obama. The growth of wireless technology. Facebook. YouTube. iPhones. And many, many other changes.

And yet, in spite of all these changes, the central thesis of this book has not become obsolete. In fact, it has become even more relevant. As we move deeper into the 21st Century, it is becoming increasingly clear that we are living in a post-product world that makes 19th Century industrial-age thinking, still used by most business people, even more obsolete.

When we first published this book in 1999, most readers were intrigued by its message, but they couldn't see the application to their business. We realized then that the new revolutionary model presented in the book—The Relationship-First Formula—was ahead of its time. We realized that only the most advanced leading-edge business thinkers would embrace this new approach. But as the years went by, and companies became more affected by accelerating change, increasing competition, and instant communication, more and more people read the book and embraced its premise.

With the dramatic financial crisis of 2008, and the subsequent global recession, this search for new ideas and models became more urgent. It became apparent that this was not just any ordinary recession, but perhaps a turning point in world economic history. We believe this is true. We believe that many product-first companies will not survive the recession, while others will continue to suffer low or negative growth. We also believe that efforts to bail out these product-first company will not work in the long-run.

But all is not lost. That is the great, positive message of this book. It is our belief that our economic future is incredibly positive. We believe only 1% of the value that could be created, has been created, and that 99% more value creation is possible. And that means 99% more wealth for everyone on the planet. But it won't be the kind of product-oriented wealth brought to us by the machines of the industrial revolution. It will be intangible post-product wealth that provides intellectual, emotional, and spiritual benefits beyond anything we can currently imagine. It will also be sustainable value that protects our planet, promotes peace, and makes the most efficient use possible of our precious and limited natural resources.

I may be idealistic in my vision of the future, but I ask you; what are the naysayers offering? Are you inspired by their vision? As I explain in this book, if we start with an ideal model, we are more likely to achieve it. So here is my contribution to a better and brighter future: Beyond Basketballs: The New Revolutionary Way To Build A Successful Business In The 21st Century.

Bill Bishop 2011

Introduction:
Building the Better Boat

At the cottage during my childhood, I learned an important business lesson observing the competition between two local boat owners—Ron and Milton—who provided water-taxi service on our lake. When you needed a boat ride, you called either Ron or Milton. It didn't matter who. They both had small, run-down boats.

Ron's wooden vessel had torn seats, and it reeked of motor oil. The engine clinked and clunked like a washing machine full of auto parts. Water oozed through the floor boards. Customers kept their life jackets on and prayed they would make it across the lake alive.

Milton's boat wasn't much better. There were no cushions on the seats. There wasn't much room for luggage. And no matter where you were sitting, you always got splashed with water spray as the boat chugged through the white caps.

Everyone complained about Ron and Milton and their pathetic boats, but they were the only game in town, and on the surface, it didn't appear competition was driving them to improve their service. It was like they had a water-taxi oligopoly. But we were wrong. Things were about to change.

Ron worked seven days a week. He kept his little boat going and going and going. His poor outboard motor reminded me of an old mule being pushed to its limit on a forced march. It was like cruelty to motors.

Milton, on the other hand, took two days off a week. He let Ron enjoy all the business he could muster on Mondays and Tuesdays.

But Milton knew what he was doing. He had a secret. On his days off, Milton was building a better boat. For three years, he worked on his new craft every Monday and Tuesday, and he designed the vessel to suit the needs of his customers. He put in luggage racks. He put in nice comfortable seats. He put in a quiet in-board motor. He also made the boat big. It could carry 10 passengers. And he made the boat fast. It could get across the lake five times faster. As a finishing touch, he put in a cooler full of juices and soft drinks.

When Milton launched his new boat, it created a sensation. Everyone loved it. Everyone, of course, except Ron. Within weeks, Ron was out of business. No one wanted to risk their life in his boat, when they could travel in style on Milton's. Soon after, a broken man, no doubt, Ron went back to work at the local hardware store.

What strategic lesson did I learn from the saga of Ron and Milton? I learned it's important to take time off regularly to plan and build a better business. By making less money in the short term, you can make much more money in the long term. You can work seven days a week, like Ron, delivering the same value over and over again, or you can take some time off like Milton to plan and build better strategies, systems and capabilities. I learned you can keep running the same small, run-down business forever, or you can devote some time to building a better business.

And that's the main reason I've written this book, Beyond Basketballs: To help you plan and build a better business in a post-product economy.

These lessons, learned long ago, also started me off on a journey of discovery. During the past 25 years, I've been a keen observer of businesses, both large and small. I'm fascinated by what makes them succeed or go bust. I've learned many companies fail to grow, or go bankrupt, because they don't stop to plan and build a better business. They're so concerned about making money in the short term, they lose sight of their future. They don't have a long-term perspective. So they never grow. They never get bigger or better.

Conversely, I've come across many successful companies that grow bigger and bigger. They succeed because they've found the balance between planning and action. They spend time delivering value, but they also spend time creating value. They are always working on a bigger boat. They develop clear strategies and design new systems in detail. They always think things through before they take action.

Most importantly, I wrote this book to explain new strategies and systems that will help you thrive in today's post-product world of accelerating change, increasing competition, and instant communication. I contend that the old strategies and systems don't work anymore. They wouldn't even work for Milton, the hero of our story. Although he beat out Ron years ago, Milton eventually went out of business himself. He couldn't keep up with all the change and competition. Now there are dozens of water-taxi companies on the lake, and boat technology has improved dramatically. His home-built boat is quaint compared with the high-tech watercraft plying the lake today.

Milton's focus on creating a better product won't work today. To succeed, it now takes much more than a better product or service, no matter what your business or industry. In today's marketplace, your business must be built around a specific type of customer, not around your products or services. It must also focus on providing non-traditional value components, mostly of an intangible nature. That's why in the first chapter of this book I explain the Relationship-First Formula. This new formula for success will help you thrive in a world that's changed almost beyond recognition since the days I took boat rides with Ron and Milton. It will help you build your own version of a better boat.

Making The Transformation

As you will see, Beyond Basketballs was written to help you transform your company from one based on the obsolete Product-First Formula to a new model called The Relationship-First Formula. It doesn't matter whether you run a one-person company in the basement of your home or a multi-national corporation. The over-arching principles are the same regardless of your company's size, industry, or structure. The models, strategies and systems are universal.

To help you make this exciting transformation to a company which thrives in an age of accelerating change, increasing competition, and instant communication, I've structured this book in a logical step-by-step format. The information is presented in the same manner and order used when my company consults to companies around the world. All of the models, strategies, and systems have been tested and successfully used by hundreds of our clients. They have been proven to work. The chapters cover the following:

Chapter 1: The Relationship-First Formula: In this chapter, I explain why the old ways of doing business don't work in an age of accelerating change, increasing competition, and instant communication. I explain the product-focus business model (the Product-First Formula), and why you need to replace it with a new business model (the Relationship-First Formula), a formula that will help you thrive in the 21st century.

Chapter 2: The Post-Product Reality: Before your company can become a Relationship-First Enterprise, you have to face up to the realities of the post-product world. You can't ignore or run from these basic facts of life. You have to accept that these realities are not going to go away. Instead, you have to change your business so you can thrive because of these realities, not suffer from them.

Chapter 3: The Performance Plateau: Companies that adhere to The Product-First Formula eventually run out of potential: They stop growing and progressing. They reach what I call The Performance Plateau. This chapter looks at the eight major reasons (called Limiting Factors) which strand companies on this plateau.

Chapter 4: The Principal Strategies: To become a Relationship-First Enterprise, you will have to make many fundamental changes in your company. You will have to adopt many new models, strategies and systems in your organization. I call these The Principal Strategies. This chapter explores them in detail.

Chapter 5: The Relationship-First Enterprise: In this chapter I provide a description of The Relationship-First Enterprise: the ideal company that thrives in an age of accelerating change, increasing competition, and instant communication.

Chapter 6: The Relationship-First Scenarios: To help you understand how to apply The Relationship-First Model, I present six hypothetical examples of different companies.

Chapter 7: The Transformation: The concluding chapter explains the step-by-step process to transform your company into a Relationship-First Enterprise. I explain each step in detail, and provide a series of tools and exercises to help you make the required strategic decisions.

The Importance of Being Earnest

I suspect many business people will not be able to shake off their industrial-age, product-first thinking. Their resistance, of course, is in your best interests, dear reader. The business people who first truly make a commitment to the principles of The Relationship-First Enterprise, will get a giant head-start. So if you're ready, begin by reading Chapter 1: The Relationship-First Formula.

> Those who will not reason
> Perish in the act:
> Those who will not act
> Perish for that reason.
> *W.H. Auden*

CHAPTER 1:
The Relationship-First Formula

> *"The Special Theory of Relativity was to give Einstein his unique position in history. This dissertation of some nine thousand words overturned man's accepted ideas of time and space and it drastically altered the classical conceptions of physics still held by the overwhelming majority of scientists..."*
>
> **Ronald W. Clark: Einstein—The Life and Times**

When Albert Einstein published his Special Theory of Relativity in 1905, he set off a revolution that changed forever our understanding of the universe. In one brilliant stroke, Einstein eclipsed Sir Isaac Newton, whose laws of motion had been the cornerstone of physics for 250 years. How did Einstein, working alone in a Swiss patent office, accomplish such an amazing intellectual feat?

Historians offer many explanations for Einstein's breakthrough, but two key reasons stand out. First, Newton's laws did not account for many things Einstein observed in nature, and he was driven to find a better way to explain the universe. He couldn't let Newton's laws go unchallenged if they didn't work. Second, young Einstein developed his theories outside the scientific and academic communities of his time, so he wasn't boxed in by bureaucratic or incremental thinking. He was free to explore radical new ideas, to think "outside the box," unencumbered by established beliefs or misconceptions.

These two factors—the need to explain the world better, and the ability to explore radical new ideas—are the driving forces behind this book. Why? For one simple reason. The old ways of doing business no longer work!

Our most cherished business models, strategies and systems, which haven't changed much since the beginning of the Industrial Revolution, are obsolete. They simply don't work in today's post-product world of accelerating change, increasing competition, and instant communication. New ideas are needed. New models. New strategies. New systems. And not just strategies and systems that build on industrial models. But totally new ones that have no link whatsoever to their predecessors. Like Einstein, we need to think outside the box.

Why am I so adamant about this? Well, because I'm not the only one who feels this way. I've worked with thousands of business people, and most of them have several things in common. They're frustrated. They're confused. And deep inside, I think, they're angry. They're angry because no matter how hard they work, no matter how much planning they do, no matter how much money they invest, something always seems to prevent them from reaching their goals. To illuminate this frustration, let's consider a hypothetical example such as Trinity Gear and Rod. (This fictional example, like all the examples in this book, borrows from real-life cases I've dealt with in my consulting practice.)

Trinity Gear & Rod: Trying to succeed in today's world

In business for more than 60 years, Trinity has had plenty of ups and downs, but it has never encountered anything like the current perplexing state of affairs. During the last 10 years, the global gear and rod industry has undergone dramatic change. With the revolution in robotic manufacturing, Trinity's customers—mostly manufacturing engineers—need a much wider variety of gears and rods, in smaller quantities, often with custom specifications. The growing demand for made-to-order, just-in-time gears and rods has cut into the profits Trinity once enjoyed on long product runs. In fact, meeting this new demand has caused Trinity's profits to stay flat for more than five years; they've hit a plateau.

To keep pace with the rapid changes in technology and in the marketplace, Trinity's engineers keep trying to come up with new innovative products, such as the exciting line of Trinity 1000 Titanium-Alloy Gear Assembly Units. However, every time Trinity Gear & Rod comes out with new products—which take about 18 months to develop—one of their major competitors, such as arch-rivals Axiom Global Gear, almost immediately come out with a better one.

Trinity has tried almost everything to combat the competition. They've lowered their prices, but the competition always matches the reduction, putting the squeeze on profit margins. They've increased their advertising and attendance at trade shows, but this has added additional promotion costs. They've even tried to branch out into other businesses, such as their disastrous foray into the aluminum extrusion industry. All of these efforts have done nothing to improve what has become a cut-throat commodity business.

To add insult to injury, many of Trinity's long-time customers have drifted away to the competition. Their customers now use the Internet to shop around for gears and rods. If they find a better price in Singapore, they buy the goods there. If they find a better rod in Brazil, they buy it from there. Everyone at Trinity complains that long-time customers have no loyalty these days; if something better comes along, they jump ship in a flash. All of their great customer service in the past seems to mean nothing in an age of cross-border shopping, e-commerce, and online auctions.

Losing long-time customers wouldn't be so bad, however, if Trinity could get lots of new customers. But that has become harder and harder to do. Trinity salespeople complain that nobody wants to hear their sales pitch anymore. Manufacturing engineers are too busy, or too jaded, to sit still for an explanation of the brilliant benefits of the Trinity 9000 Series of Vicosity-Enhancing Gear Pins. "I can't even get them to return my calls," complains Trinity's most seasoned salesperson.

To make matters worse, the cost and complexity of Trinity's operations keeps going up. They've armed themselves with all of the latest and greatest gizmos: enterprise-wide software, lightning-fast processors, neural networks, Internet servers, satellite uplinks and downlinks, computer-driven assembly, just-in-time distribution, and one of the most elaborate websites in the industry. But all of this technology has cost a lot of money, and a lot of it is already outdated. It also takes a huge team of people to keep all of the machines humming and working together. There are constant glitches, crashes, and system errors. Even when the system is working, it's frustrating to use, because every department at Trinity has its own technology and its own ways of managing information. Very little information can be shared from department to department. As a result, Trinity employees are frustrated by the existing system, and spend most of their time trying to piece together fragmented and incomplete information.

In spite of these obvious drawbacks to the benefits of technology, Trinity's technologists have advised senior management to keep upgrading their systems or perish. But a lot of people at Trinity suspect new technology won't be the answer to their problems. They also suspect they need to do something completely new with their business, but there's no consensus on what to do, or how to start.

The problems and difficulties confounding Trinity Gear and Rod are being experienced to some degree by virtually every business today, in the traditional manufacturing sector, the service sector, or even in the new high-tech and digital age industries. All are trying to succeed in a world beset by accelerating change, increasing competition, and instant communication.

So what's the solution? Well, the first step is to understand why business people are so frustrated. I believe they're frustrated because they're using an out-moded equation for success. I call this equation The Product-First Formula, which is stated as:

$$\textbf{Product } (P) \times \textbf{Large Number } (LN) = \textbf{Success } (\$)$$

People use The Product-First Formula because it's the only equation for success they know, and because it makes a very compelling promise: If you have a product and you sell a lot of it, you will make a lot of money. It's so simple. Come up with a great product. Make the same product over and over again. Sell it to a whole lot of customers. And rake in the money. That's all there is to it. (Note: I'm not just talking about companies that sell tangible products, but services as well. The equation could also be called The Service-First Formula.)

Companies that follow this formula have several things in common. First and foremost, they start all strategic thinking with their product. If they want to grow their business, they begin by asking: How can we make our product better? Should we make it a different color? Should we make it bigger? Smaller? Can we make it cheaper? Should we distribute it differently? Should we position it differently in the consumer's mind? Or maybe we should make another product. Maybe we should start another business and make something else altogether. Or maybe we should merge with one of our competitors.

Companies that use The Product-First Formula are also obsessed with the competition, and as the competition increases, they become even more obsessed. They spend a lot of their time wondering: What's our competition doing? How can we make our products better than theirs? Should we lower our prices to beat them? Should we buy them out? Should we get them to buy us out?

As well, companies that follow The Product-First Formula build all of their strategies and systems around their products. These systems—built to accommodate product-related functions such as engineering, manufacturing, distribution, and finance—can become seriously fragmented and ineffective when applied to creative and relationship-building activities such as sales and marketing.

Whether consciously or unconsciously, most companies in the world today use The Product-First Formula because it has worked for almost 200 years, ever since the beginning of the Industrial Revolution. There are three reasons why it has worked:

Slow Rate of Change: The world didn't change very quickly in the

19th century and for most of the 20th century. If you made shoes, you could sell a large quantity of the same shoes for many years. Market conditions stayed basically the same for decades. Fashions, technology, laws, regulations and other important issues in your business changed, if at all, at a glacial pace. You could go along for years, even decades, producing the same product in large quantities without changing your business in any significant way.

Limited Competition: Second, The Product-First Formula worked during the Industrial Age because in those days there was comparatively little competition. If you manufactured cars, there were few other companies in the same business. If you sold insurance, there were only a couple of other insurance companies. If you ran a hotel, there were very few other hotels to compete with. The lack of competition gave you the ability to produce the same product or service over and over again without any additional investment in product development. With little competition, you also had more power to set the price and maintain a high profit margin.

Uninformed Consumers: And third, The Product-First Formula worked because producers had more information than consumers. During the Industrial Age, consumers did not have the incredible access to information they have today. It was usually difficult or impossible for consumers to compare prices or look at alternative products. They didn't know if better shoes were selling for half the price across town. It was pretty difficult to get across town too. Consumers' lack of knowledge allowed you to maintain your profit margins, and helped you sell more of the same product over and over again.

These three conditions—a slow pace of change, relatively little competition, and uninformed consumers—are necessary for The Product-First Formula to work. Without them, the formula collapses. If everything keeps changing—market conditions, consumer tastes, technology—you have to keep changing your products and services. If competition increases, the consumer will see very little difference between your products and competitors' products. This will force you into a commodity trap where the only variable is the price. In a commodity trap, your profit margin will drop precipitously, sometimes below zero. And finally, if consumers can get information quickly and easily about all of the products or services in a particular category, the downward pressure on profit margins will intensify. All of these factors make it virtually impossible to maintain a healthy profit margin while producing a large quantity of one product over and over again.

In the world we are living in today, change is accelerating at a dizzying pace, global competition is mounting, and knowledgeable consumers can shop around on the Internet from the comfort of their homes or offices. In today's marketplace, the three conditions necessary for The Product-First Formula to work no longer exist. Simply put, the formula is outdated, and all of the efforts of a company to make it work—price wars, line extensions, retail promotions, advertising campaigns, sponsorships, websites, new technology, strategic alliances, takeovers, and mergers—will ultimately prove futile.

Given the changes going on in the world today, why do people still cling to the old Product-First Formula? For two reasons. First, the formula has been ingrained in our culture for so long, most of us aren't aware we're even using it. And second, if we are aware of using the formula, and have an inclination to change it, the embedded strategies and systems supporting the outdated formula often present a seemingly insurmountable barrier.

Both of these conditions—lack of awareness, and an inability to change—are fraught with danger. Companies that continue to base their business on The Product-First Formula will have less success in the future. As the pace of change increases, it will become harder to make a profit on any particular product. As competition increases, it will be more difficult to get out of the commodity trap and maintain a high profit margin. As consumers use the Internet more and more to shop for the best prices and products, the profit margins of businesses will be squeezed even more.

In this environment, new technology or a change in consumer tastes can put you out of business overnight. At the very least, you will waste an inordinate amount of time, money and effort trying to make an old formula for success do new tricks. And remember, I'm talking about any kind of organization—software companies, travel agencies, small businesses, government agencies, associations, consulting firms, and major corporations—that start all of their strategic thinking with their products or services.

So what's the solution to this problem?

We need to throw out The Product-First Formula and adopt an entirely new business model: The Relationship-First Formula.

The Relationship-First Formula

To thrive in this age of accelerating change, increasing competition, and instant communication, we need to cast off 19th century thinking and adopt a business model more appropriate for the 21st century. This new way of thinking, The Relationship-First Formula, is stated as:

Quality Relationships (QR) x **Unique Value** (UV) = **Success** ($)

This formula has one over-riding principle: Instead of building your business around products or services, you build it around a specific type of customer. The mission of your business is to provide this type of customer with a steady stream of unique value. All of the strategies, processes, and systems of your company are designed to deliver this value, and to foster a long-term relationship with this type of customer. I call this kind of company, a Relationship-First Enterprise.

Why does The Relationship-First Formula make more sense for the times we live in?

A Relationship-First Enterprise works better because it thrives in an environment of change, competition, and instant communication. It takes advantage of change because its relationship-first strategies and systems allow it to instantly seize new, unforeseen, and highly profitable opportunities.

A Relationship-First Enterprise does not worry about the competition, because it doesn't have any competition. It stands out as unique in the customer's mind because it provides him or her with a continuous and ever-expanding stream of Unique Value. As well, because it has a completely integrated information system—built around its customers, not its products or services— A Relationship-First Enterprise uses instant communication to its advantage: to deepen its relationship with customers and prospects.

To illuminate the difference between these two business models, let's take a look at two fictional companies—one that still uses The Product-First Formula, and another company that transformed itself by employing The Relationship-First Formula.

Syntax Switching: Caught in the Product-First Trap

For 40 years, Syntax Switching had been a world leader in the telephone switching industry. Founded in 1952 by Dr. Emmett Syntax, a brilliant engineer and scientist, Syntax Switching led the way in the development of innovative switches for telephone companies, and private telephone exchanges. As profits grew steadily through the '70s, '80s and '90s, the company built more than 20 different manufacturing and product development centers around the world. The number of employees also grew at the same pace.

Then in the late '90s, the company reached a plateau in sales revenue, and profits began to drop as foreign competitors entered the marketplace. Prices fell sharply for switching equipment. As the pace of technological innovation sped up, Syntax Switching was forced to bring out new products more often. The average product life cycle contracted from an average of three years in the 80s to less than three months in the late '90s. In addition, customers began asking for customized switches, and they didn't want to wait months or weeks for delivery. But Syntax's business systems were not set up to handle custom orders efficiently. The sales people were becoming frustrated because the assembly plant couldn't meet the expectations of their customers.

To make matters worse, the launch of the company's new line of switches—The Galactic Switch Series—was a dismal failure. By the time the new products were ready for market, the telephone industry had adopted a standard protocol incompatible with the new product line. No one at Syntax Switching was willing to shoulder the blame for the gaff. After all, who could have predicted two years earlier that the industry would change its standards?

Things were looking bleak for Syntax Switching, even though the global telecommunications industry was growing at an astounding pace. Sales for the company were flat, and employee morale had hit rock bottom. People were quitting in droves because the place was such a depressing and unpleasant place to work. The remaining staff were frustrated by the company's fragmented computer system. A productivity audit revealed the people in the company spent, on average, more than 80 percent of their time on low-value mechanical activities, and less than 20 percent of their time dealing directly with customers.

In an attempt to address the problems plaguing Syntax, senior management convened an emergency weekend conference at a golf resort. The executives talked endlessly about the future of the industry, where switching technology was headed, and what new innovative equipment they could build to keep up with the competition. Very little mention was made of the company's customers and prospects, because most of the senior executives didn't know them very well. At the end of the session, the company decided to develop another line of switches—The 5200 Quasar Interchange Series—based on some exciting new innovations developed by Syntax engineers. The senior executives were excited by the potential of the new product line, but some of them harbored secret reservations that it would not succeed when introduced 18 months later. They were right. The company went into receivership.

The Basketball People: A Relationship-First Enterprise

Very few people remember the days when The Basketball People only sold basketballs. That was back in 1999, when Bouncy Basketballs Incorporated was one of the top five basketball manufacturers and distributors in the world. During that year, management at Bouncy Basketballs realized they had to change their business model or they were headed for bankruptcy. The air had gone out of the market for basketballs, and sales were flat. Competition had increased as low-priced basketballs bounced on to the market from overseas. After reading this book, the president of Bouncy Basketballs, Horatio Hoop, decided to drop the company's Product-First Formula (basketballs), and adopt the Relationship-First Formula.

The first step in the company's transformation was to choose its target customer type. That was simple: basketball players. Horatio Hoop and his team decided to build their business around *basketball players* instead of *basketballs*. Although it seemed simplistic, this single decision completely changed the destiny of the company.

By focusing on *Basketball Players*, the employees began to think creatively for the first time in many years. They asked themselves: "What Unique Value can we deliver to *Basketball Players*? "What do they need and want?" The first answer was easy: "We can sell them basketballs, that's for sure." Well, what else? "We could sell them basketball uniforms, basketball training videos, basketball team management software, and information about professional basketball players. We could also bring basketball players together by sponsoring tournaments or online forums. We could sell basketball trophies, backyard basketball hoops, and even build basketball courts. And if we are really successful, we could buy a professional basketball team."

All of these ideas made Horatio Hoop and his team really excited about the future of the company. After all, no matter how much the world might change in the future, there would likely always be *Basketball Players*. This was something the company could rely on in a world awash in change. They could also stop worrying about the competition, because basketball sales would only be a small part of their business. As well, their new Relationship-First approach would breathe life into their website, which had languished for years as an expensive electronic brochure.

To launch the new direction, the company changed its name to The

Basketball People, and published a book called *The Essential Basketball Player's Handbook*. The book was available free in print and e-book formats to anyone who registered on The Basketball People website, or at one of more than 2,000 retail locations. All of the information gathered from the book promotion was entered into the company's people database. Over an 18-month period, detailed information was gathered from more than 750,000 basketball players, including their e-mail addresses.

During this time, The Basketball People began building the world's most extensive website on basketball. The site included statistics on all professional NBA teams, tips from pros, free software for managing a basketball team or tournament, basketball training manuals, listings of sport injury clinics, discussion forums, online basketball play-off pools, and The Basketball People Store, which featured the basketball-related products sold by more than 5,000 vendors. No matter what you wanted to buy, if it was about basketball, you could get it from The Basketball People.

Over a period of five years, The Basketball People has built a relationship with more than 15 million basketball players around world. A massive amount of information is known about each individual player. This information is used to create even more interesting products and services for them. Using e-mail and The Basketball People Web-TV channel, the company is able to communicate quickly and easily with every player in its database.

What's more, by putting basketball players at the forefront of its thinking, the company developed an information system centered around its customer database. Seamlessly integrated, and based on a component organizing principle (see Chapter 7: The Transformation), the system allows The Basketball People to create new products and services in a matter of days. If a new opportunity arises, the organization can quickly sort, process and deliver a completely unique package of products and services.

By adopting The Relationship-First Formula, the company has grown exponentially. It never runs out of new ideas for innovative products and services. There is no competition: in fact, some of its former competitors now sell their products, for a fee, on The Basketball People website. Profit margins run well above average. Revenues have grown by more than 1,000 percent. But the true sign of success occurred just recently, when The Basketball People sold off its basketball manufacturing division. "It wasn't profitable for us to manufacture them anymore," said one of the company's executives at the time of the sale. "Now we will just sell them while someone else makes them."

A Tale of Two Formulas

The differences between Syntax Switching and The Basketball People are many, but a few distinctions stand out. While Syntax Switching continued to focus its strategic efforts on its products, The Basketball People made the switch to The Relationship-First Formula.

In many ways, the change in strategic focus set The Basketball People free. They were free to think creatively about how to help basketball players get a lot more out of the game. They were free of their narrow "basketball" mindset. They were also liberated from their fear of change, their obsession with the competition, and their blind faith in the power of technology to solve their problems. And they were able to start listening to and learning from their customers.

The people at Syntax Switching, on the other hand, sadly never made the switch. They went out of business moaning and groaning about how fast the world was changing, about how the competition was really unfair, and about how the Internet and all that other technology ultimately wrecked their business.

In the final analysis, the tale of these two companies is clear: one became a Relationship-First Enterprise, and the other did not.

My Moment of Enlightenment

Like all of us, I once lived under the spell of the Product-First Formula. Back in the late 1980s and early 1990s, I was very excited about new computer technology for building online bulletin board systems (BBSs). At that time, before the mass popularization of the Internet, BBS systems were all the rage. I started a company that built BBS systems for associations, magazines, and corporations. My dream was to sell BBS subscription services to as many people as possible.

For a while, I thought I was on my way to fame and fortune. I had thousands of people signed up. The keys for the Rolls Royce were waiting. Unfortunately, the dream never materialized. The day the World Wide Web rolled onto the scene was the day everyone lost interest in hearing about bulletin board systems. I had been steamrolled by new technology. My previously enthusiastic clients cancelled their BBS subscriptions without apology and signed up immediately with an Internet Service Provider. Almost overnight, the BBS business was put out to pasture.

This devastating setback compelled me to do some serious soul searching. What had I done wrong? Then it hit me. I had built my business around a product and a very specific type of technology. Obviously, I realized later, a new technology was going to come along and change everything. But while I was enjoying success, I didn't keep my eyes open. In many ways, I was afraid to look at what was happening outside my doors because I had invested a lot in BBS technology. I didn't want to think about what might wreck my dream.

When I realized the folly of my product-first focus, I thought about how to build a business that would be more future-shock resistant: A business that wouldn't be dependent on the vagaries of technology for success; a business that would thrive in an age of accelerating change.

I started thinking about my customers. What was I trying to do for them? I had been trying to help them succeed in their business using digital technology. Helping my clients really didn't have anything to do with BBS systems per se. In fact, I had been trying to sell BBS systems to people who didn't really need them. I had been so obsessed with my own product, and my own dreams, I had completely lost touch with what my customers really needed. As a result, I had completely ignored the arrival of the Internet and the World Wide Web.

That's when it came to me. If I built my business around my customers (business owners), I could provide them with whatever they needed to succeed in their business. If they needed a BBS system, great, but if they didn't, then I would help them in some other way.

That was when the creative floodgates opened. There were hundreds of things we could do to help business people use technology more effectively for their business. From that moment on, our business exploded. We wrote books, gave workshops, made speeches, conducted audits, and built marketing systems using dozens of different technologies. And most important, our customers started to succeed as well. By taking off our product blinders, we could see exactly what our customers really needed to help them succeed.

That's when I realized we had entered a post-product world, where success would be based on relationships, not on products.

CHAPTER 2:
The Post-Product Reality

"I am certain that none of the world's problems have any hope of solution except through all of the world's individuals becoming thoroughly and comprehensively self-educated. Only then will society be able to identify, and inter-communicate, the vital problems of total world society. Only then may humanity effectively sort out and put those problems into an order of importance for solutions that will work for all life on Earth."

R. Buckminster Fuller

Futurist, global thinker and inventor of the geodesic dome, Buckminster Fuller devoted his life to solving the world's problems. His approach to global problem-solving, called "Comprehensive Anticipatory Design Science," looked at each specific issue—such as hunger, resource depletion, environmental degradation, and militarism—in the context of a total system. Only by taking this "big picture" perspective, Fuller contended, is it possible to devise new models, strategies and systems to solve these global problems.

To become a Relationship-First Enterprise, you and your company must also look at your problems in the context of a global post-product system. You must face up to the realities of the world we live in today: a world characterized by accelerating change, increasing competition, and instant communication. You need to acknowledge that these realities are not transitory. They are not aberrations. The world has changed fundamentally since the Industrial Age, and we will never return to the conditions of the past. You must either face up to these realities and change your business models, strategies and systems accordingly, or go out of business. It's that simple.

So, the first step is to face the post-product realities head on. Although there are many trends, issues, and facts associated with today's global economy, I have identified eight fundamental realities that have a significant impact on virtually every business. They are:

1. The rate of change is accelerating
2. Commodity margins are collapsing
3. Consumers rule the marketplace
4. Prospects are harder to reach
5. Markets and channels are fragmented
6. Product life cycles are shrinking
7. Technology plays a pivotal role
8. Existing markets are not enough

Let's look at each of these in detail.

Reality #1: The rate of change is accelerating

In our world today, everything is changing faster and faster. In every area of our lives—personal, political, economic, cultural, technological, spiritual—we are being swept away by a tidal wave of change. But things are not only changing; the pace of change itself is changing—it's accelerating. Instant global communication is increasing the flow of new ideas, symbols and images. Newer, faster, smarter computers are speeding up the development of new technologies. And the global clash of different cultures and societal norms is accelerating the demand to change virtually every institution and tradition.

This "speeding up" of our world, or in the words of Buckminster Fuller, this "accelerating acceleration," is causing what Alvin Tofler called "Future Shock." Every day, we wake up and we wonder: "What's next? What change will take place today that will force us to restructure our life and our business?"

Ironically, as the pace of change accelerates, more consultants, pundits, gurus and futurists seem called upon to predict the future. You can't pick up a newspaper or magazine, watch television, listen to the radio, or browse the Internet, without coming across an expert who tells you what the world will be like next month, next year, or in the decades to come. And this trend is not limited to the media world. Most companies, big or small, are populated by people who make it their business to predict the future. They prophesize and pontificate: "Next year, our market will grow by 50 percent. This technology will be used in every household five years from now. Our competitors will introduce this kind of product in the next three years. We need to install these kinds of computers, and this kind of software. They will be the standard technologies in the next decade. We need to build our business around this product because consumers in the future are going to want it."

All of these prognostications are an attempt to bring some semblance of order to a chaotic world, to make an uncertain future more certain. But this kind of fortune telling is a dangerous game. Why? Because accelerating change means you can't predict the future. It's impossible. In fact, if someone makes a prediction, bet against it. There is a greater chance the prediction won't come true. It's simple logic. In a world with so many variables—millions, perhaps billions of variables in each situation—how can anyone claim to predict the future? As the Monty Python gang says: "Nobody expects The Spanish Inquisition!"

The thing is: all companies using The Product-First Formula run their businesses based on predictions about the future. They decide to develop a specific product because they predict it will be needed in the future. They put in new computers, software and equipment because they think these technologies will make the company more competitive in the future.

These decisions, of course, could be wrong, and in an age of accelerating change, they are likely to be wrong. And this is the key point. Strategic decisions based on a prediction of the future—no matter how much supporting research has been amassed—will probably be wrong. And that's why so many companies these days are frustrated by the accelerating pace of change: Their entire organization—its models, strategies and systems—has been designed based on predictions. And when the future doesn't turn out as expected, their organization is unable to change and adapt.

So what's the alternative? It's simple. Instead of trying to predict the future, face up to the fact that you have no idea what the future will bring. Be confident you don't know what will happen. Don't build your business around a prediction of the future. Build it so it has the ability to adapt quickly to profitable but unforeseen opportunities as they arise. In this way, you won't be afraid of change, you'll welcome it. Every change will be seen as an opportunity, not as a huge transport truck that slams into you when you're not looking.

A Relationship-First Enterprise is a company designed to take advantage of change. All of its models, strategies and systems are based on the principle that you can't predict the future. You can only prepare to seize new opportunities as they come up. In upcoming chapters, I will explain new models, strategies and systems to transform your business into a Relationship-First Enterprise, and take advantage of the accelerating pace of change.

Reality #2: Commodity margins are collapsing

In our global economy, profit margins on commodities keep falling. In fact, they are collapsing. The amount of profit you can make selling a commodity keeps dropping. And I'm not just talking about traditional commodities such as oil, bauxite or pork bellies. A commodity is any product or service considered by the consumer to be the same no matter who is selling it. This now includes personal computers, financial products, long distance telephone calls, air travel, consulting services, basketballs, charitable causes and hundreds more.

If you sell a product or service that is basically the same as your competitors, you are in a commodity business, and your only competitive strategy is to lower your prices. The only way to make a profit is to become more efficient or cut costs, or both. As the number of your competitors increases, there is even more pressure on you to lower your prices. Because your customers can use instant communication technology to learn exactly who has the best price in the marketplace, you are under pressure to lower prices again. Within a short time, the difference between your costs and your price (profit margin) is almost nil. This may sound like Economics 101, but wait. In today's global economy things get even worse.

In many industries, companies are giving away commodities for free in order to initiate a long-term relationship with customers. Telephone companies now give away free telephones, and even free telephone service to get new subscribers. Companies give away computers, Internet service, e-mail, software, and other commodities. In these cases, the price of the product is zero! There isn't any profit margin at all. It's actually a negative profit margin. The question is: If one of your competitors starts giving away a product almost identical to yours, where does that leave you? Who knows what might happen in the future (I certainly don't!), but we might see companies give away free cars or houses in order to sell customers something more valuable. If this happens, I wouldn't want to have a business selling cars or houses. I wouldn't be able to compete at any price!

Companies that sell a commodity and find their profit margins under constant pressure are caught in The Commodity Trap. Because they make a very small profit on each sale they have very little money left over to invest in innovative research or more effective marketing systems. They also don't have the incentive to spend quality time with customers. After all, if they only make a few pennies on each sale, they can't afford to spend much time with each customer. They aren't worth it. As well, there is no incentive to add additional value or quality to the product. You can't afford it. All of these factors push the company further and further into The Commodity Trap.

Companies based on The Product-First Formula are destined to fall into The Commodity Trap. Hoping to sell a large number of the same product, these companies will have no option but to lower their price as new competitors enter the marketplace. They may even price their product below cost in an attempt to drive competitors out of business.

In most cases, these strategies will fail, and keep the company fixated on their product, and caught forever in The Commodity Trap.

The Relationship-First Enterprise, on the other hand, never falls into The Commodity Trap. By providing its customers with a steady stream of Unique Value, The Relationship-First Enterprise has no comparable competition. No competition means no price competition. The Relationship-First Enterprise can then set the price it thinks the market will bear without worrying whether it will be slashed by competitive forces. Its customers, who have a Quality Relationship with the company rarely shop around or compare prices. Committed to their relationship with you, they are willing to pay a fair price for the value they receive. In this way, The Relationship-First Enterprise enjoys the benefits of a healthy profit margin, and it can use the extra money to invest in innovative ideas or to foster more quality business relationships. It can also use the profits to invest in capabilities that will allow it to seize even better opportunities in the future, which will, in turn, generate even more profits. I call this state of continuous upward progress, made possible by a healthy profit margin, The Profit Margin Multiplier. It is the exact opposite of The Commodity Trap. (In the next chapters, I will explain models, strategies and systems that will help you break out of The Commodity Trap and take full advantage of The Profit Margin Multiplier.)

Reality #3: Consumers rule the marketplace

When I was working on my previous book, **Global Marketing for the Digital Age**, I spent a lot of time writing at my neighborhood coffee shop. Terence, the owner of the shop, had enjoyed brisk business for more than 10 years. He asked me: "Why should I worry about globalization? I've got lots of loyal customers in this neighborhood, and I'm not interested in opening other shops around the world. I don't think globalization has anything to do with me."

At first I thought he had a point. I knew globalization was increasing competition in just about every industry, but maybe a small business person like Terence was immune. His customers were fiercely loyal.

His cafe was a second home for many of them. No matter what happened, he would always be able to count on his hard-core caffeine-crazed clients. But Terence and I were wrong. In the next six months, three franchises opened cafes in the neighborhood. At first, Terence's customers pledged their allegiance, swearing they would never imbibe their latte or espresso in enemy territory. But slowly, over time, many of them drifted away to the new cafes, attracted by the lower prices and higher quality coffee. Terence's revenues and profits fell sharply, and the atmosphere of community, which had made the cafe so appealing, waned. The long arm of globalization had claimed another victim.

Terence's transnational tale has a number of lessons for us all, but one is paramount. In our age of cross-border competition, product-based consumer loyalty is dead. The days are behind us when you could count on your customers to stick with your products through thick and thin. Today, when a better product or service comes along, your customers will probably flee like vermin from a sinking scow. When there is a dramatic difference in currency rates, your country's consumers will gaily scamper across the border to pick up bargains, leaving local merchants in the lurch. If a new technology hits the market, customers will quickly abandon their existing equipment for new glittering gizmos.

Why has consumer loyalty disappeared? I believe there are two reasons.

First, consumers are no longer loyal because most producers have never bestowed any loyalty on them. In spite of empty proclamations to the contrary, most companies treat their long-term customers no better than someone who just walked in the door. Worse, they often take loyal customers for granted, focusing all their time and energy on getting new business.

Second, consumers lack loyalty today because they are much more powerful than producers. It's consumers, not producers, who dictate the terms of the marketplace. During the Industrial Age, the opposite was true. In those days there was a limited number of producers, and people were starved for products. Producers set the price, the delivery date, the terms of the warranty (if any), and dictated what options were available (if any). In the Industrial Age, producers had the upper hand, but today, consumers rule the marketplace. They have virtually unlimited choice. They have increasing access to market information. They are more sophisticated and global in their tastes. And they are more fickle. If something better comes along, today's consumer will seize it in an instant. They simply want the best combination of quality and price, and they don't care where they get it, or from whom. If they can get a better price in Tanzania, they will shop there. If they can get better quality in China, they'll go there. After all, it's only business, right?

The rising power of consumers over producers has significant consequences for every business. If your business is centered around products, your turn-over in customer relationships will increase. If your customers only have a relationship with you because of your products, they will abandon you the moment they like someone else's product better. They won't give you a second chance. Losing customers will be inevitable for any product-centric company. In an age of constant change, fleeting consumer tastes, and leap-frogging technology, something better will always come along sooner or later to tempt away your customers.

The Relationship-First Enterprise, however, does not worry about the increasing power of consumers. In fact, the mission of The Relationship-First Enterprise is to give consumers even more power: To empower them: To give them more choice: To give them more information: To keep up with their changing tastes and moods. The Relationship-First Enterprise empowers consumers by developing a long-term relationship with them based on the delivery of an on-going stream of Unique Value (UV). No matter what customers want, The Relationship-First Enterprise is dedicated to helping them get it. If the customer wants the competitor's product, The Relationship-First Enterprise helps him get it. If the customer wants to buy something in Mozambique, The Relationship-First Enterprise is the one that enables the long-distance transaction. The Relationship-First Enterprise is there whenever its customer needs help, information, advice, or a capability. The more power The Relationship-First Enterprise can give the consumer, the better. As a consequence, The Relationship-First Enterprise thrives because of more powerful consumers, not in spite of them.

Reality #4: Prospects are harder to reach

People often ask me to describe the difference between sales and marketing. In my parlance, selling is a ***dynamic*** activity: a salesperson proactively makes cold calls or knocks on doors. Marketing, on the other hand, is an ***attractive*** activity. Instead of having to make cold calls, the marketer <u>receives</u> calls from prospective customers. The marketer doesn't need to knock on doors, because people are coming to him or her.

Given a choice, I would rather be a marketer than a salesperson. I would rather have customers come to me, than spend the rest of my life trying to get reluctant people to listen to my sales pitch. I don't want to end up like Willy Loman, the woeful protagonist in the play, Death of a Salesman.

Surprisingly, most companies invest the lion's share of their time, effort and money on sales and very little on marketing. In an on-going survey conducted by my company, we found the average company spends about 80 percent of their effort on sales, and 20 percent on marketing.

Why is there such an emphasis on sales when it seems obvious that marketing is a more ideal situation? Three reasons.

First, most companies focus on sales because sales can yield results much faster than marketing. If you make cold calls, or knock on doors, you might make a sale right away.

Second, most companies focus on sales because they view marketing as a cost. They think money spent on advertising, publicity, newsletters, websites, trade shows and other marketing tools is an expense, a necessary expense perhaps, but an expense nonetheless. With this marketing-as-an-expense mentality, the company's natural instinct is to minimize marketing costs. As a result, these companies are more willing to spend money on sales, even though it can be shown that marketing is actually less expensive over time.

Third, the picture of the dynamic salesperson going from door to door is one of the most enduring icons of the Industrial Age. It's a fable that goes like this: When a company invents a great product, the salesperson embarks on an heroic quest to find customers. After many trials and tribulations, our battle-weary salesperson returns home with sales in hand to a warm welcome. This fable has been with us for almost 200 years, it seems almost incomprehensible that we would abandon it. That's why questioning the role and effectiveness of the sales function is sacrilegious in many companies.

In today's global economy, however, the age of the salesperson is over. Prospective customers are simply harder and harder to reach. Increasing numbers of salespeople complain it's more difficult to get through to prospects. They can't get prospects to listen to their sales pitch. But why is that? To understand this problem, let's look at it from an historical perspective.

In the Industrial Age, people were more willing to take the time for a sales pitch. The pace of life was slower. The amount of information being communicated was playing at a much lower volume. Consumers were less inclined to stop salespeople from calling them, or visiting them. Lacking information, people actually wanted to hear a sales pitch. The heyday of the Industrial Age was the golden age of the salesperson.

Conditions today are, of course, significantly different. Wherever they turn, consumers are constantly bombarded by sales messages, whether through television, radio, magazines, newspapers, movies, the Web, e-mail, direct mail, billboards, telemarketing, or through social media. As a result, consumers today suffer from sensory overload, and their only defense is to block out any unnecessary sales pitches.

As well, consumers today have less time than their Industrial Age counterparts. At home and office, consumers run full tilt. They don't have a lot of time to hear a sales pitch. They are also jaded. They think they've heard it all. They've sat through so many sales pitches, they have become adept at cutting through all the sales mumbo-jumbo.

Finally, consumers today, out of self-defense, have lots of tools to block out your sales pitch. They've got channel-changers, private voice-mail, call-display, e-mail filters, and personal assistants trained to turn away pesky salespeople. Ironically, as salespeople use technology more to reach prospects, consumers are using technology more to block them out.

Recently, I experienced just how hard it is for companies today to reach consumers. While I was shopping at the local supermarket, a young woman with a clipboard approached me and asked, "Would you be willing to take 20 minutes to answer a survey about our store?" With two kids, a business to run, and a very hectic schedule, my answer was obvious: "No, I don't have 20 minutes for a survey. Even if I did, what's in it for me? What do I get for giving you all sorts of valuable information about myself?" Those questions took her aback, but she answered gamely: "Well, in the future, it'll mean you'll get better service from us." I was impressed by her quick thinking, but not by her answer. They were asking me to give them something of value (information about myself) in exchange for some nebulous value in the distant future.

As I went on my way, I thought: "Why don't they offer me a $20 discount on my groceries, or something else of value? Isn't the information they want from me at least that valuable?" By not offering me any value, the company did not get through to me. Like a salesperson, the survey person was not able to reach me, a prospect, because I was too busy, overwhelmed, and jaded, to fill out another research survey.

The growing barrier between you and your prospects has serious implications for every business. If you cannot communicate your sales message to prospects, you cannot develop new business relationships. As sales prospects become harder to reach, you will become increasingly isolated in your business. All of your efforts to make your sales pitch will become more frustrating, expensive and futile.

Companies clinging to The Product-First Formula will be especially hard hit by this trend. The more these companies focus on their products, the more they will be inclined to continue making sales pitches. They will continue to drone on about their products and how they are better than the competition, and consumers will tune out even more and become harder and harder to reach.

In today's global economy, the sales pitch is no longer an effective way to start new business relationships. Something else has to take its place. The answer, once again, is quite simple. In order to "attract" people to your company, you have to give away value during the initial sales and marketing process. I call this Attractor Marketing. Instead of making a dynamic sales pitch, you provide something of real value to the prospect to entice them. The greater the value you provide, the more attracted they will be to you. After all, you are the one who is trying to initiate the relationship, so it's your job to offer prospects something valuable at the outset. If you just give them a sales pitch, they probably won't be interested. If you give them something of value, they will be more interested. (In coming chapters, I will explain this marketing concept in more detail.)

Reality #5. Markets and channels are fragmented

In the Industrial Age, there was one market for your products (the mass market), there were a few ways to distribute your product, and a few places to promote your product. A marketing plan was a simple document. In today's global economy, creating a marketing plan can be a nightmare. There are thousands of potential markets, myriad methods of distribution, and a plethora of promotional possibilities. For a company based on The Product-First Formula, this fragmentation of markets and channels is just another frustrating example of a world gone mad.

To cope with the fragmentation of markets and channels, business people now embrace the concept of Segmented Marketing. They talk more about market "segments": distinct clusters of customers defined in a certain way, such as **Wealthy Investors**, **Homeowners**, or **Parents**.

The purpose of segmented marketing is to select a distinct group of customers, identify their special needs, and cater to those needs with unique "segmented" products, distribution channels, and promotional vehicles. For example, a university might create a special educational workbook for parents. They would take their existing educational material and pull together a custom-tailored workbook for parents. They would distribute the workbook through stores that cater to parents, and promote it through magazines and websites aimed at parents.

Many companies attempt segmented marketing, but most of them are ill equipped for the task. That's because all of their strategies and systems are based on The Product-First Formula. For example, let's look at Trinity Gear & Rod, the company we first met in Chapter 1. Designed around The Product-First Formula, Trinity started by developing the new line of Trinity 1000 Titanium-Alloy Assembly Units. Then it turned to its marketing department and asked it to find some customers.

The marketers developed a sales brochure for the new line and sent it out to their customers and prospects: manufacturing engineers. The reception was lukewarm, so they decided to target two sub-segments: ***Auto-Parts Manufacturers*** and ***Consumer-Products Manufacturers***. Then they decided to go even further and sub-divide the first segment into ***Large Auto-Parts Manufacturers***, and ***Medium-Sized Auto-Parts Manufacturers***. For each of these segments, Trinity created custom-tailored products, chose unique distribution channels, and put unique ads in different trade magazines catering to each group.

The company's segmented marketing program was progressing perfectly until orders started coming in. Most of the customers were looking for custom orders. They wanted titanium-alloy assembly units that matched their particular specifications. When these orders were sent to the manufacturing plant, all hell broke lose. The staff, the equipment, and the company's computer systems were simply unable to handle the volume of custom orders. Delivery dates were extended, and then extended again. Costs mounted as product runs got smaller. Anger and frustration spilled over onto the shop floor. The sales people were furious. Customers were disappointed. Quality suffered. In Trinity's case, the Global Reality of fragmented markets and channels crashed into the company's outmoded product-centric systems.

Trinity's story (based on dozens of real-life cases with which I'm intimately acquainted), demonstrates the predicament faced by the majority of companies today. As they move from mass marketing towards segmented marketing, their strategies and systems become increasingly outmoded, and they are totally ill-equipped for the ultimate form of segmentation (one-to-one marketing). They are not able to create customized products for each customer. They are not able to handle individualized distribution channels, or pull together individualized promotional programs.

The Relationship-First Enterprise, on the other hand, is designed to thrive in a world of fragmented markets and channels. Its strategies and systems allow it to deliver Unique Value to each individual customer. The Relationship-First Enterprise has abandoned the concept of specific products, and has embraced the concept of Value Components. All of its products, services, ideas, information, and capabilities have been distilled into individual Value Components. The company's mission is to constantly add more components of value for its designated Customer Type. Its systems enable customers to assemble these components easily using instant communications technology. In this way, The Relationship-First Enterprise recognizes that markets and channels will continue to fragment until every person constitutes a unique market, with their own unique distribution channel, and unique method of communication. (In coming chapters, I will explain how you design strategies and systems to help you thrive in an age of fragmented markets and channels.)

Reality #6. Product life cycles are shrinking

During the Industrial Revolution, the idea of a product "life cycle" was unknown. Products produced in the 19th century and early 20th century—such as shoes, ice-boxes, shirts, cars, candy bars—had a seemingly unlimited life span. Producers could pump out the same product year after year with few modifications or changes.

The notion that a product had a limited life span, or a life-cycle, only emerged in the last few decades in response to the three major trends of the Global Reality: accelerating change, increasing competition, and instant communication. Each of these trends shortens the length of time a product can last in the marketplace. Companies are forced to adapt their products to keep up with new technology, new ideas, and new consumer trends. Competition compels companies to constantly improve and repackage their products and services. And instant communication feeds the consumer's appetite for the exotic and the novel. Obviously, in today's marketplace it's no longer possible to just keep running with the same product, month after month, year after year. You have to come up with something new every year, every month, every day, every hour, every minute.

Shrinking product life-cycles is a frustrating reality for companies using The Product-First Formula, because their organization is designed to handle long product runs (Large Number), not short runs. Their systems are not configured to handle the rapid birth, growth, maturity, and death of a product. Every time they have to launch a new product, chaos ensues. They have to overhaul their production equipment, their computer systems, their marketing materials, their distribution methods, and their sales pitch. It's like trying to get a huge ocean liner to perform like a powerboat.

As we move deeper into the 21st century, product life-cycles will continue to contract until every product is a unique product, every order is a custom order. Product life-cycles will be zero. The concept of a product life-cycle will become obsolete. In this world, any company designed around The Product-First Formula will also become obsolete. It will be unable to produce unique products quickly enough to meet customer expectations or with enough profit to keep its operation viable.

Let's shine a spotlight on the reality of shrinking product life-cycles. Consider the case of Ziggurat Incorporated, one of the world's leading makers of personal computers. As a pioneer of the computer industry, Ziggurat has enjoyed a leadership position in the PC market for decades. It has built an efficient system for the development, manufacturing, distribution, and marketing of personal computers. It launches and markets a new line of PCs every 18 months. Customers can buy Ziggurat's computers through selected retailers, through computer consultants, or by using Ziggurat's state-of-the-art website.

To most observers, it appears Ziggurat has its act together, but during the past five years, the company has faced stiff competition from an upstart firm called Progenitor PCs Incorporated. Consumers have flocked to Progenitor because it offers custom-built PCs, delivered within a few days, at incredibly low prices. Someone looking for a PC can access the Progenitor website and assemble a PC that matches exactly their individual requirements. Progenitor warehouses are specially designed to bring together all of the components requested by the customer, and ship the completed PC quickly out the door.

Progenitor's just-in-time, one-to-one business model has shaken the rafters at Ziggurat Incorporated. When consumers learned they could build their own individual computers at Progenitor, they became less interested in Ziggurat's already-assembled PCs. Ziggurat responded by coming out with new computers more often (by shrinking its product life-cycle), but this was not enough to please the savvy PC buyer. They wanted to build their own.

Ziggurat considered adopting Progenitor's business model, but the company's product-centric systems were simply too well established to change easily. Its distribution network, for example, consisted of more than 100 warehouses across the globe. The warehouses were built to store and ship large numbers of the same kinds of computers to retailers. They were not designed to assemble and ship custom orders direct to consumers. In addition, Ziggurat's other systems—manufacturing, finance, and marketing, and the entire culture of the company—were not capable of handling custom orders. With such firmly entrenched strategies and systems designed around The Product-First Formula, Ziggurat Incorporated was powerless to match the swift-footed systems employed by Progenitor.

Ziggurat's quandary teaches us two things. First, no matter how well Ziggurat can shorten its product life-cycles, it won't be enough to meet the customer's demands for individual orders delivered quickly and economically. Second, if your company's strategies and systems are built around The Product-First Formula, you will have to overhaul them to operate effectively. Your systems must be designed based on The Relationship-First Formula. Your systems must allow you to deliver Unique Value on an individualized basis and still make a profit. (In coming chapters, I will explain how to envision and build this kind of system in your company.)

Reality #7: Technology plays a pivotal role

During the Industrial Age, most businesses operated in a linear fashion. Each stage followed the next: market research, engineering, manufacturing, promotion, sales, distribution, finance, and customer service. As projects passed from one stage to the next, each department would handle the assignment in its own unique way. The manufacturing department would use its own processes, and its own technology. The marketing department would use completely different processes and technology. And so on. Companies could thrive even though each department was like a different country, with its own unique culture and language.

In today's business environment, this linear business model has become obsolete. Since the advent of networked computing, business has become a spatial, not linear, process. All business processes happen simultaneously. To succeed, departments must work together, share information, and be part of a team. That's why the role of technology has become so pivotal. If you have a well designed Information Technology system, you will have a greater chance of success. You will be able to deliver more Unique Value faster, better, and in a more individualized way. If you have a poorly designed IT system, you'll have a harder time delivering Unique Value, and you won't be able to seize new profitable opportunities as they arise.

The pivotal role played by technology in business today is apparent to me when we conduct a strategic systems audit of a company's Information Technology (IT) system. We determine how well their company's technology supports its marketing objectives. We ask: Does the system allow the company to communicate quickly and easily with its customers? Does the system allow the company's staff to spend most of their time on High-Value Activities (Creating and Delivering Value)? Or do the staff spend most of their time on Low-Value Activities (such as the mechanical gathering, processing and distribution of information)? If staff members spend the majority of their time on Low-Value Activities, the IT system is inadequate. If the staff can concentrate most of their time on relationships and creativity, the system works.

Our audits reveal, however, that most companies have poorly designed IT systems. The systems are often seriously fragmented. Different databases that can't talk to one another are scattered across the company. Different software is used in different departments. Sharing data across the company is impossible. This fragmentation seriously undermines the productivity of the company, and limits its ability to respond quickly to change.

From our audits, we have deduced three reasons why most IT systems are fragmented. The first reason has historical roots. Before the age of networked computing, most PCs were standalone units. As computing became more important, each department began to develop software tools to handle specific tasks. These tools became the nervous system of the department. When it became possible, and necessary, to network together all of a company's computers, the systems in each department clashed. It is only natural that they did not work together. It was as if feudal fiefdoms, long isolated from one another, were suddenly forced to become part of a much larger nation state. Battles broke out to determine which standard would be adopted, which software protocol would be used across the company. And of course, each department vigorously defended its own way of doing things. So nothing was done. There wasn't enough leadership at the top to bring all of the IT systems into line.

The second reason why most IT systems are fragmented is that they are built around specific technologies. I call this The Technology-First Approach. Using this approach, a company chooses a particular type of software and hardware and proceeds to build its systems around it. The problem with The Technology-First Approach is that the overall objectives and strategies of the company play second fiddle to the technology. The potential of the technology determines the potential of the company. And conversely, the limits of the technology determine the limits of the company. In this environment, technologists become the masters, and the company's strategists become mere followers. As well, by designing their systems with a product focus, technologists leave customers almost entirely out of the equation, except, perhaps, as an entry on an invoice.

Technologists also have a hard time making the leap from a product-focus to a customer-focus. That's because product-centric IT strategies stress efficiency, making things go faster for less money. Customer-centric strategies, on the other hand, must be based on relationships, not efficiency. And relationships sometimes take longer and cost more. To thrive in an age of accelerating change, increasing competition, and instant communication, The Relationship-First Enterprise designs its technology around its customers, not around its products. Its systems help them develop Quality Relationships with their customers by increasing the amount of time they can spend on Creating Value and Delivering Value, and less time on Low-Value Activities.

The heart of the system is their People Database that acts as the company's collective memory. The database keeps track of their customers and prospects, and records their comments, their preferences, their needs, and their transactions. The database system allows them to communicate with their customers through e-mail, Facebook, YouTube, by telephone, or through whatever future technologies emerge. The system also allows them to deliver Unique Value to their customers by facilitating the quick and easy assembly of their Value Components.

It also gives them the capability to seize new opportunities as they arise. (In coming chapters, I will explain how to design an IT system which supports The Relationship-First Formula, and I'll give you ideas on how to help your company's technologists understand and support the need to build IT systems around customers, not products.)

Reality #8: Existing markets are not enough

During the Industrial Revolution it was possible to prosper serving only your local market. Protected by trade barriers, your turf was free of foreign competition. You could produce a Large Number of your Product without having to venture beyond your own borders. In today's global economy, however, your local market is buzzing with competition due to the globalization of trade and the proliferation of instant communications technology. In addition, many companies now face competition from outside their own industry. Insurance companies, for example, are now competing against banks. Telephone companies now compete against cable services. Coffee shops now compete against bookstore cafes.

In this competitive environment, if you stick to your existing market, your share of that market is bound to keep falling. That's why you must face up to the eighth reality: Existing markets are not enough. You must think globally. Fortunately, it's now possible for every business to expand its market perspective. Thanks to the Internet, even a one-person business can attract and serve customers around the world. By providing Unique Value to a well-defined Customer Type, The Relationship-First Enterprise is ideally suited to thrive in the global marketplace.

A company with College Students as its customer type, for instance, can serve them around the world. Linguistic and cultural differences aside, College Students have much the same needs no matter where they live. They require help with their studies, financial assistance, and a job upon graduation. They also need to have fun while they're in school, and participate in a community of other college students. As such, there is virtually an unlimited number of ways The Relationship-First Enterprise can deliver Unique Value to College Students, no matter what country they live in. In fact, The Relationship-First Enterprise does not need to factor national boundaries into its thinking at all. That issue is irrelevant. The Relationship-First Enterprise's market is College Students and on a global scale, this market is huge.

Companies based on The Product-First Formula have great difficulty making it in the global marketplace. Because they operate in a commodity business, and start all of their thinking with a product, they tend to brush aside the peculiarities of foreign markets. They have trouble grabbing market share from indigenous competitors who know the local market in more detail. And they usually fail to develop long-lasting quality relationships with foreign customers. In most cases, they simply haggle over the price, settle for what they can get, and ship the product.

Companies based on The Relationship-First Formula however, fare much better. That's because it's possible to run a viable business on a global scale serving almost any Customer Type, no matter how rare or unusual, such as Bonsai tree growers, emu farmers, brain surgeons, Edsel owners, Polish film fans, or physically-challenged scuba divers.

Ironically, the more focused you become, and the more specialized your chosen Customer Type, the greater your ability to deliver Unique Value. This strategy—Customer Type Specialization—is a powerful way to reach out and build Quality Relationships with foreign consumers. (In upcoming chapters, I will explain how to move beyond your existing markets, and put in place models, strategies and systems that will help you thrive in the competitive global economy.)

Facing Up To The Post-Product Reality

Most business people are aware of these eight realities, but they don't take action to change their strategies and systems accordingly. They secretly hope the world will revert to the golden age of the Industrial Revolution. Their resistance to change is not caused by a lack of will; they just don't know how to cope with these realities. They don't know how to become a Relationship-First Enterprise. That's why I wrote this book. I want to help you design a business that will thrive in the world as it is today. But before I outline the blueprint for The Relationship-First Enterprise, it's necessary to move from the macro to the micro perspective and examine the internal reasons why many companies become stranded on what I call The Performance Plateau.

CHAPTER 3:
The Performance Plateau

"Without freedom from the past there is no freedom at all, because the mind is never new, fresh, innocent. It is only the fresh, innocent mind that is free. Freedom has nothing to do with age, it has nothing to do with experience; and it seems to me that the very essence of freedom lies in understanding the whole mechanism of habit, both conscious and unconscious. It is not a question of ending habit, but of seeing totally the structure of habit."

J. Krishnamurti

J. Krishnamurti, the world-renowned spiritual teacher, believed human beings could not be free until they totally understood how habits—both good and bad—drive their actions. The same idea holds true for companies. Although your business is profoundly affected by the three external conditions of the post-product reality— accelerating change, increasing competition, and instant communication—there are also many internal conditions holding you back that come from within yourself. These are the attitudes, practices, and habits for which your company alone is responsible. In this chapter we will look at these internal barriers to success, that I call Limiting Factors, which can stop your company from achieving its full potential.

The Performance Plateau

When a company reaches a certain level of performance in sales and profitability, it often becomes stuck at that level. Sales and profits remain stagnant over an extended period of time. New customers become harder to get, and many old customers fall away. The fast growth of the past is replaced by an atmosphere of low energy and ennui. I call this the Performance Plateau.

Companies become stuck on this plateau because they continue to use business models, strategies, and systems no longer appropriate for the larger organization they have become. To rise above this plateau, a company must adopt the new strategies and systems of a Relationship-First Enterprise.

To fully appreciate how your company can become a Relationship-First Enterprise, you must first understand the eight Limiting Factors that could strand your company on the Performance Plateau:

1. Focusing on short-term goals
2. Working as individuals or small groups
3. Thinking only about products and services
4. Trying to beat the competition
5. Focusing on sales, not marketing
6. Creating tools for specific situations
7. Being a slave of technology
8. Focusing only on existing markets

Let's look at each of these Limiting Factors in detail.

Limiting Factor #1: Focusing on short-term goals

Short-term thinking is a key symptom of a company stuck on the Performance Plateau. Executives, salespeople, employees, and shareholders focus solely on achieving better monthly or quarterly results. Under this pressure, the company tries to get more out of the same engine, an engine that may not have enough horsepower for the task. Caught in the rush to achieve short-term goals, the company does not take the time to install a bigger, better, or more powerful engine, and by over-stressing the old engine, performance falls as the old workhorse breaks down. Companies stuck on the Performance Plateau are simply unwilling to take the time needed to install a bigger, better engine. As a result, significant change or breakthroughs are rarely achieved.

The characteristics of a company undermined by short-term thinking are numerous. Short-term organizations:
- Focus primarily on achieving monthly or quarterly goals;
- Have no long-term vision of success for their company;
- Make major decisions and radical changes based on temporary setbacks;
- Make only small investments in new capabilities and resources;
- Take few risks, and have little tolerance for mistakes;
- Only show interest in customers and prospects with money to spend in the short term.
- Make little effort to develop deeper, more long-term relationships;
- Strive to increase sales and profitability by doing the same things, only faster, more often and better.

In order to rise above the Performance Plateau, a company must address the issue of short-term thinking. It must adopt principles and technology that enable it to think long term as well.

Limiting Factor #2:
Working as individuals or small groups

As an organization grows in size, it becomes increasingly more important for everyone to work as a team, and ironically, teamwork becomes increasingly more difficult. In many cases, the existing structures, strategies and communications systems within the company do not support efficient teamwork. Individuals and departments, therefore, tend to work in isolation from each other. Lack of teamwork keeps the organization stuck on the Performance Plateau because:
- there is no shared goal or vision. If goals are developed, they are created by a small group of senior executives;

- few employees are aware of, or understand, the major goals of the company;
- each individual or department has a different idea of what is important, and what is a priority on a day-to-day basis;
- the lack of teamwork often leads to internal competition and animosity;
- individuals and departments develop their own systems and technologies, and become fiercely territorial when there is an effort to standardize these systems across the company;
- there is no mechanism or structure for bringing everyone together;
- many departments or individuals become far removed and isolated from the real business of the company (i.e. serving customers);
- the company does not benefit from the creative power of team planning and execution.

To rise above the Performance Plateau, the organization must develop new strategies and structures for working together as a team.

Limiting Factor #3:
Thinking only about products and services

In a company stuck on the Performance Plateau, most thinking begins first with products and services. This type of company adheres to the Product-First Formula. While paying lip service to market research, the company begins the strategic planning process with a product in mind, either something new or an improvement on an existing product. After many months or years of product development, the company enters the marketplace and tries to find customers. Often, it is surprised to find people are not interested in its product. It tries to make the most of the poor market reception by lowering the price and by spending aggressively on promotion.

By starting first with a product, companies take a big risk. They spend a lot of time and money in the hope that the world will love their product after it has been developed. It's like aiming a gun, and firing a bullet at a target that won't appear for six months or a year. It's almost impossible to hit the target.

A company stuck on the Performance Plateau tends to think products first because it was a product, or line of products, that gave rise to the company's initial success in the marketplace. At some point in the past, the company created a product that found willing customers. The company grew because it was able to find more and more customers who wanted the product. And because the company only had a small number of customers, it was much easier to understand the modifications and improvements needed to keep them happy.

However, as the company became bigger, it became harder to maintain close contact with customers, and the company grew increasingly product-focused, and even less customer-focused. This problem is quite common among companies run by engineering and high-tech professionals who have had success selling a particular product in the past. It is very difficult for them to break out of this product focus, and they are especially ill-prepared when the product is no longer popular.

To rise above the Performance Plateau, companies must become less product-focused, and put the customer first.

Limiting Factor #4: Trying to beat the competition

Trying to beat the competition is often the obsession of companies languishing on a plateau. By defining itself in relation to the competition, the company tries almost anything to get one up on its rivals, through lower prices, sales, premiums, special offers, outlandish promotions, and the like. This fierce competition tends to "commodify" the company's products and services, which severely squeezes profit margins. Limited by the meagre proceeds of a thin profit margin, the company cannot maneuver in the marketplace and become a unique player. There is simply no money, or energy, to invest in innovative thinking.

A competitive focus can also adversely affect the quality of the company's products and marketing efforts. With a thin margin, there is little incentive or ability to produce a quality product for such a low selling price, or to devote enough money to mount an effective promotional campaign. A competitive focus also makes it difficult for the company to differentiate itself and its products in the minds of the customer. In such a situation, the company's products are viewed as exactly the same as the competition, or ranked as either superior or inferior. The customer never sees the company or product as a unique entity.

In addition to these pitfalls, this kind of company has little energy left to come up with innovative ideas, or to do something entirely original. By constantly trying to beat the competition, the company is destined to remain in a horse race forever. In most cases, a competitive focus means the company will always be a follower, never a leader. To become a Relationship-First Enterprise, a company must abandon its obsession with the competition and see itself as a provider of Unique Value to a unique Customer Type.

Limiting Factor #5: Focus on sales, not marketing

Most companies stuck on the Performance Plateau focus on sales, not marketing. To find new customers, such a company relies almost exclusively on the use of sales tools and methods such as telemarketing, direct mail, sales presentations, request-for-proposals (RFPs), trade shows, and promotional gimmicks. While proactive sales activity has a role in every company, a sales focus is limiting if it is not complemented by more long-term marketing activities. While sales is a dynamic process (whereby the company actively seeks the attention of a prospect), marketing at its most effective attracts prospects of their own accord to the company.

A sales focus also has an important impact on the type of relationships the company has with its customers. Under the sales model, the company is the first to initiate the relationship, which puts it in a weaker power position. The customer can always say: "You came to me in the first place. I never really wanted to be in this relationship." Under the marketing model, the prospect is the first one to initiate the relationship. Because they came to you in the first place, you have a much more powerful position in the relationship. You can always say: "You were the one who came to us, and this is how we do business."

Focusing entirely on sales can also negatively affect your business relationships, because sales people often become anxious and impatient to make a sale in order to meet a looming quota deadline. They may push customers into an inappropriate sale, and thereby threaten the long-term quality of the relationship. Salespeople working on a quota system tend to jump prematurely to the sales pitch and forego relationship building with the prospect. The sales quota bias, therefore, often results in short-term, small-dollar customer relationships.

In contrast to the established perception, sales campaigns are also much more expensive over the long term than marketing campaigns are. However, most companies stuck on the Performance Plateau never invest in marketing long enough to realize this, so they become stuck in the sales cycle. To become a Relationship-First Enterprise, you must use marketing techniques to attract prospective customers who meet your Customer Type profile.

Limiting Factor #6: Creating tools for specific situations

With its short-term sales focus, a company languishing on a plateau tends to focus primarily on the development of tools. These are tools—such as marketing materials, software programs, forms, and processes—designed for a specific event or situation. Thus, they can quickly become obsolete. As each new occasion arises, the company has to create completely new tools, usually at great expense.

This kind of company fails to invest enough time, money, or resources to develop long-term capabilities: people, technology, and resources that allow the company to take advantage of exciting opportunities. Capabilities of this nature include computerized manufacturing equipment, relational database systems, in-house design and digital production facilities, internal website design and hosting capabilities, and multimedia presentation expertise/equipment. As well, these capabilities include internal and external people who know how to take advantage of new marketing technology.

For example, the production of a new brochure (a tool) is a common activity in most companies. Countless hours and dollars are spent to develop a professional and effective brochure. Once it's printed, the brochure immediately begins to lose its value as the company and the marketplace change and evolve. Within months, the brochure becomes obsolete, and in many cases, is abandoned. (In an even-worse scenario, the company feels compelled to stick to an obsolete marketing message until the brochures are depleted!)

A Relationship-First Enterprise invests in people and technology that allow it to create custom brochures and marketing materials on a constant basis. As the company and the market changes, this kind of company can quickly develop custom tools for each specific opportunity. In this way, there is little wasted time or money, and the company has the flexibility and power to develop better relationships more quickly. It is also better able to adjust to the constant changes taking place in the competitive global economy.

Limiting Factor #7: Being a slave of technology

As technology becomes more prevalent in our national and global economies, the effective use of technology plays an increasingly critical role in the success, or failure, of a company. However, the increasing importance of technology gives many companies the mistaken notion that new technology will be the answer to all of their problems. If sales are falling, new computers are installed, and upgrades to software are implemented. If staff costs are too high, employees are let go and replaced by voice mail. If a competitor launches a better website, the company builds an even more elaborate website. In this techno-crazed environment, any new technology, no matter how unproven, is adopted on pure faith.

Under pressure to keep up with the accelerating pace of technological change, senior executives often relinquish an inordinate amount of power to their computer and technology experts. Without clear direction from upper management, the technologists earnestly install new technology with little understanding of how it will help the company achieve its primary business goals. In fact, the development of new technology can become the primary goal of the company—sometimes the only goal. By subverting the company's true goals, the blind worship of technology can have a devastating impact on the company's relationships with its people (customers, employees, suppliers, and shareholders). Because technology is viewed as the answer to every problem, it's often introduced to replace staff, or to eliminate person-to-person contact with customers. I call this problem *Technopia* (see my book *Strategic Marketing for the Digital Age*).

The worship of technology, and the resulting enslavement of the company by technology, is a common hallmark of a company stuck on the Performance Plateau. Ironically, the technology that is supposed to help the company grow is the reason why the company is unable to grow. The Relationship-First Enterprise, on the other hand, is the master of its technology. All of its systems are designed solely to deliver Unique Value to its customers and prospects. No technology is introduced unless it serves that aim.

Limiting Factor #8: Focusing only on existing markets

Many companies on the Performance Plateau are stuck because they have not found customers beyond their traditional geographic, demographic, or vertical markets. Focusing on local or existing markets is limiting because:
- there are not enough potential customers in your local market for unique, specialized products and services;
- consumers are increasingly less loyal to local suppliers;
- falling trade barriers, the digitization of the world economy, and other trends of globalization are increasing competition in all national, demographic, and vertical markets;
- industries are converging, bringing new competitors into your industry;

- global competitors have a strategic advantage due to better economies of scale, and lower labor costs;
- you are more vulnerable to downturns in your regional or national economy;
- it does not allow you to develop more sophisticated structures and systems by dealing in more varied markets.

For these reasons, a Relationship-First Enterprise must move beyond its local or existing markets to thrive in the competitive global economy.

CHAPTER 4:
The Principal Strategies

"Finally we shall place the Sun itself at the center of the Universe. All this is suggested by the systematic procession of events and the harmony of the whole Universe, if only we face the facts, as they say, 'with both eyes wide open.'"
Nicolaus Copernicus

Before Nicolaus Copernicus published *De Revolionibus Orbium Celestrium* (On The Revolution of the Celestical Spheres) in 1543, everyone believed the Earth was the centre of the universe. They thought the sun, the stars, and the other planets, revolved around the Earth. Copernicus challenged this belief, or paradigm, and proposed a heliocentric model that placed the earth in orbit around the sun. Copernicus died shortly thereafter, so he did not witness the controversy unleashed by his radical theory, or its eventual vindication.

Like Copernicus, you need to challenge deep-seated business paradigms, and adopt new ones more appropriate for the 21st century. You have to ask yourself: "Does the universe really revolve around my company and its products? Should we continue to build our strategies and systems around our products, or should we use a different model?" If you have read the previous three chapters, you know the answer to these questions. In our age of accelerating change, increasing competition, and instant communication, you need to become a Relationship-First Enterprise by building your business around a specific Customer Type using the Relationship-First Formula. And I'm not just talking about adopting relationship marketing strategies, or improving customer service. I'm talking about designing your entire business—from top to bottom—around a clearly defined type of customer.

Transforming your company into a customer-centric enterprise may be a challenge of epic proportions. If your company has well-entrenched models, strategies and systems designed around products, the bias against change will be formidable. Consider what you are facing. Products may have to be discontinued. Marketing programs may have to be abandoned. Expensive software systems may have to be trashed. People may have to be laid off, or shifted into new roles. And most significantly, old ways of thinking will have to be questioned and rejected if they prove to be outdated. All of these changes will be resisted by some people in your company no matter how obvious it is that change is necessary.

However, to help you with this transition, I have identified eight new Principal Strategies, which if adopted into the culture of your company, will help you make the changes necessary to become a Relationship-First Enterprise. The Principal Strategies are:

1. Start with a Customer Type
2. Don't compete; provide Unique Value
3. Deliver Unique Value through teamwork
4. Envision ideal system models
5. Give away value to start Quality Relationships
6. Offer components of Unique Value
7. Develop capabilities, not tools
8. Go down before going up

Principal Strategy #1: Start with a Customer Type

A Relationship-First Enterprise, built around customers, not products or services, starts all strategic thinking by choosing a specific Customer Type. The Customer Type can be general, such as *parents*, or *windsurfers*, or *retired people*, or it can be very specific, such as *parents with handicapped children, professional female windsurfers,* or *rich retired people who like to trade stocks on the Internet.* In fact, the more specific you are about your Customer Type, the easier it will be to begin and foster a long-term relationship with them.

For example, let's say you are a travel agent. In the past, you built your business around your products: travel packages and airline tickets. From the customer's perspective, you sold a commodity, and your travel agency was just one of hundreds in your city. To attract business, you had to keep lowering your prices, and your margins. Using the Relationship-First Formula, however, you decide to choose a specific Customer Type such as *jazz music lovers*. You build your business around *jazz music lovers* by providing them with incredible Unique Value such as packaged tours to international jazz festivals, and boat cruises with famous jazz musicians. Your website, The Jazz Music Travel Centre, which provides travel information for every jazz festival in the world, is a magnet for thousands of *jazz music lovers* around the globe. They learn about your website because you promote it on dozens of popular jazz sites, through advertising in jazz magazines, and through your sponsorship of jazz events. In a short time, your travel agency becomes the premier source of travel services for jazz lovers around the world.

If this business is lucrative enough, you can stick with this one Customer Type, or you can expand into other Customer Types. (You can think of this as Customer Type Extension, in contrast to Product Line Extension.) For example, once you've established *jazz music lovers* as a Customer Type, you can choose another one, such as *wine lovers*, and build another business around them. You can market tours to vineyards and wine festivals around the world. Once again, *wine lovers* will seek you out because you are the only company catering to their specific wine-related travel needs. All of your competitors are simply travel agencies that don't understand the specific travel interests of wine lovers.

Of course, once you've established your Jazz Music Lovers business, and your Wine Lovers business, you can expand infinitely by choosing more Customer Types: *surfers, harmonica players, divorcees, Picasso fans, gourmet food lovers, antique car owners, dog owners, short people, tall people, history buffs.*

The point to remember is: Each Customer Type is a separate business. In the customer's eyes, there is no overlap. The *history buff* doesn't run into dog pictures when he comes to your website. The *surfers* don't see *antique cars* in your *surfers* brochure. However, that doesn't mean you can't use the same resources and capabilities for each company. For example, your online payment system can be used for all of your Customer Types, and you may need only one office to handle all of your Customer Types, especially if most of your business is done over the telephone or the Internet. In other words, you can increase your return on investment by using your existing capabilities to provide Unique Value (UV) to more Customer Types.

Starting with a Customer Type has an impact on every facet of a Relationship-First Enterprise. Once you have chosen a type of customer, it's much easier to make strategic decisions. As you develop Quality Relationships with customers who match your designated Customer Type, you will learn more about what Unique Value they need and want. There will be no more guessing. You will only create new products or services if your customers want them. You will also learn quickly how to attract new prospects to your company, and what processes and marketing tools work best to start and foster long-term relationships.

As well, you will bring on only the new people, capabilities, and technology that will allow you to increase the Unique Value for your Customer Type. You won't get sidetracked by flashy new technology, or the fast talk of management consultants. Your formula for success will be simple. If something provides Unique Value to your Customer Type, it will be useful. If it doesn't provide this value, it won't be useful. In this way, starting with a Customer Type will make your company more focused; help you dramatically cut down on wasted money, time, and effort; and set out a clearer path for the future of your business.

Starting with a Customer Type helps you develop Quality Relationships with customers and avoid the dangers of the Product-First Formula. For example, let's say you sell a product custom-designed for construction companies called Bull-Dozer Software. With your product foremost in your thinking, you make sales pitches extolling the product's unbeatable features. You talk about its power, its flexibility, and its expandability. You love your product, and when prospects offer resistance or express a concern, you bulldoze through them with slick retorts and exaggeration. Focused solely on your product, you do all the talking, and do very little listening. You don't listen, because you might find out customers don't need your product or that your product isn't very good.

You might realize the customer should buy Edifice Erector, a software program sold by your competitor. You can't face the truth, so you don't listen. In fact, you don't really care about the best interests of your prospects. You just want to make a sale, even if it is the wrong thing for your customers. This attitude, which stems from your Product-First mindset, makes it impossible to develop a long-term Quality Relationship with your customers.

On the other hand, let's say you are a salesperson who uses the Relationship-First Formula. Instead of making a sales presentation, you begin each call with an open mind; without a preconceived idea about how you will help them. You begin each call by finding out as much as possible about the person's situation. "What are your goals? What have you accomplished so far? What is your next challenge? What are your needs?"

From this fact finding, you use your experience and creativity to craft a unique solution for the customer. You might recommend that the customer combine components of Bull-Dozer Software with components of Edifice Erector. You might explain an innovative process that helps construction companies increase productivity by 50 percent. You might provide interesting articles and access to additional resources and capabilities, even if they come from outside your company. Instead of being obsessed with your product, you are unbelievably helpful. You are committed to having a Quality Relationship with customers by doing whatever it takes to help them achieve their goals.

Finding out what the customer needs first has been a staple tactic used by many companies in the past few decades. However, most companies pay lip service to customer research. Originating from the Product-First Formula, their customer research is actually a sham. These companies are just pretending to listen to customers. They are just trying to come across as interested in the unique needs of their customers. But behind this show is their real agenda: to sell their product. That's why so many companies ignore or disparage information gleaned from focus groups or consumer research projects. They only want to get positive feedback. They don't want to listen to the real concerns of customers because that might require them to make some dramatic changes to their business.

So don't comfort yourself with the fact that you conduct focus groups and ask your customers to fill out a survey. If you start your thinking with your product first, you are just kidding yourself. You are behaving like a pickpocket: when he looks at people, all he sees is pockets.

Starting with a Customer Type is the most important Principal Strategy because it affects everything about your company. If your company adopts this Principal Strategy, you will free yourself from the bondage of the Product-First Formula. You will expand the potential of your company a thousand-fold. You will free up the creativity of your organization that has been enslaved by product-centric thinking. You will be like Copernicus; when he realized the sun did not revolve around the Earth, he was able to see the reality of the universe, with his eyes wide open.

The Three Key Concepts of Principal Strategy #1:
1. Start all strategic thinking with a specific Customer Type.
2. Build your business by delivering Unique Value to your designated Customer Type.
3. View each Customer Type as a separate business.

Principal Strategy #2:
Don't Compete; Provide Unique Value

The mission of the Relationship-First Enterprise is to deliver an ever-increasing level of Unique Value to its designated Customer Type. Committed to this mission, the Relationship-First Enterprise leaves behind the world of competition because the Value it provides is Unique. By delivering customized solutions from a host of Value Components, this kind of enterprise no longer suffers from the falling margins of the commodity trap. Its customers do not compare its products and prices with competitors, because there is no way to make a comparison. By fostering Quality Relationships through the delivery of Unique Value, the Relationship-First Enterprise takes itself out of the competitive rodent race. In fact, the Relationship-First Enterprise transforms its former competitors into potential customers and strategic partners.

To illustrate this concept, let's pretend your trucking company chooses *restaurant owners* as its Customer Type. In the past, you had more than 200 competitors in your market area. Now you don't have any competition because you provide restaurant owners with Unique Value through your Total Restaurant Delivery Program. The mission of the program is do whatever you can to help Restaurant Owners with the acquisition, delivery and management of the food and materials in their restaurants.

For example, in addition to deliveries, you have also developed dozens of innovative processes to help *restaurant owners*. You coordinate the just-in-time delivery of fully prepared meals from remote locations. Your Total Restaurant Delivery Website enables restaurant owners to purchase their food and materials online, and keep track of their costs. You've also developed unique packaging methods that speed up the time it takes to get frozen foods into restaurant freezers. Working with an insurance company, you've created The Total Restaurant Insurance Program, which insures *restaurant owners* against the damage and theft of their inventory.

And this is just the tip of the iceberg lettuce. You are constantly developing new ways to provide Unique Value to *restaurant owners*. To this end, you've teamed up with 20 of your previous competitors to develop a much larger fleet of delivery trucks. These companies now pay you every time their trucks are used as part of the Total Restaurant Delivery Program.

As you can see, the potential of your trucking company soared the moment you took your eye off the competition and made the commitment to provide Unique Value.

To further understand the importance of providing Unique Value, consider this example. Suppose you run a telecommunications company. You sell a compendium of products: telephones, long-distance calling, mobile and wi-fi wireless telephone service, business answering systems, Internet access, and products such as call answer, call display, and three-way calling. You have a bounty of products, but you also have a bounty of competition. In every product category, you are in a cut-throat struggle, battling it out by lowering your rates, or by offering special promotions. This competitive playing field has blurred the impression your company makes on your customers. They tend to lump you together with your competitors because you all seem to be the same. They don't think there is anything unique about your company or its products. If they can get a telecommunications service cheaper from someone else, they often make the switch. You are caught in the Commodity Trap, and you know it's just going to get worse as the global telecom industry becomes even more competitive.

Your challenge is to differentiate yourself from your competition, and develop more Quality Relationships with your customers and prospects. To accomplish this goal, you choose *small business owners* as a customer type. You create The Small Business Telecom Solution, a complete program to help business owners maximize their use of telecom and online technology. You launch the program by inviting *small business owners* to a free Small Business Telecom Webinar. At the webinar, your expert speakers explain strategies and technological ideas to help small business people succeed. Importantly, you never mention your products or services during the seminar. You are just there to help people. Following the seminar, the prospects are invited to join The Small Business Telecom Club. Membership entitles them to a free e-mail newsletter, a personalized account on your website, discounts on long distance telecom rates, and a free mobile telephone. During the webinar, you get to know the participants better by asking them questions about their goals and their business.

Following this initial introduction, you go to the prospect's office to conduct an audit of their telecom systems. You go in without any preconceived ideas, and from the research, you pull together a customized package of telecom-related Value Components. The custom package includes telecom integration strategies, call centre technology, Internet access services, wireless capabilities, and advanced software solutions. Some of these Value Components are provided directly by you, and others are provided by your former competitors. In fact, you are prepared to offer your customers access to any kind of Unique Value, no matter who provides it, as long as it helps your customers succeed in their business.

As you can see from both of these examples, if you provide Unique Value, the concept of competition is irrelevant. You don't have any, and ironically, your competitors suddenly become potential suppliers of additional Unique Value. You can even make money from work done, or products and services produced, by your former competitors. Furthermore, by acting as the conduit of Unique Value to your customers from an unlimited supply of sources, you can't help but strengthen your Quality Relationship with them. Because you don't represent any special interest, or promote a hidden product-centric agenda, you are the first person the customers call when they need something. They know you will be the best person to provide them with the Unique Value they require.

The Three Key Concepts of Principal Strategy #2:
1. Exit the competitive arena by providing Unique Value and by developing Quality Relationships with designated Customer Types.
2. Provide Unique Value by expanding the range and scope of the value you create and deliver.
3. Transform your competitors into strategic partners or customers by providing Unique Value.

Principal Strategy #3.
Deliver Unique Value Through Teamwork

Individual initiative and creativity are a vital part of every enterprise, but in today's business environment, Teamwork is essential. Teamwork allows The Relationship-First Enterprise to bring all of its effort and resources into alignment in order to deliver Unique Value to its designated Customer Type. Teamwork results in more focused thinking, greater productivity, less duplication of effort, and higher levels of motivation and enthusiasm.

Unfortunately, Teamwork is sadly lacking in most of today's organizations, especially those companies built around the Product-First Formula. In these companies, people, strategies, and systems don't work together; they are severely fragmented. For example, in a typical product-centric company, the manufacturing department uses one type of information system, while the marketing department uses another. Information cannot be shared easily between these two departments. If there is a desire to combine the two distinct systems, there is usually a clash, like two feudal armies opposing each other on the battlefield. No one wants to give up their system. No one budges. There is no teamwork. In this environment, delivering Unique Value is almost impossible.

Fragmentation of this kind is common in many other areas of product-centric companies. Often the company communicates a fragmented marketing message. Each marketing tool—brochure, website, e-mail newsletter, advertisement, presentation—says something slightly different about the company. If you ask 100 employees to describe what their company does, you get 100 different answers. Every time someone makes a sales presentation or a speech, the message comes out differently. Once again, the message being communicated is not consistent, because everyone is working in isolation. Usually the graphic identity of the organization is also fragmented. Brochures look different from websites. Fax cover sheets look different from stationery. Logos are displayed in 10 different ways, all slightly different.

When it comes to the gathering, processing, and storage of information, fragmentation can be a chronic malady. Paper-based information is scattered across the organization, waylaid in different filing systems, under people's desks, in distant storage rooms. Digital information is scattered across hard drives, servers, and networks. Finding information is time consuming and stressful. Often the information cannot be found, and when it is, it's often inaccurate or incomplete. Re-filing the information poses a dilemma, because there is no common system. Everyone has their own way of doing things.

On a strategic level, fragmentation is a serious problem in product-centric companies. In most cases, the engineering/manufacturing department uses completely different models and strategies from the sales/marketing department. As we saw in the case of Trinity Gear & Rod (see Chapter 1, "The Relationship-First Formula"), the sales force was eager to meet the demands of customers for more customized products, while the engineers pushed for more standardized products. The engineers were using the Product-First Formula by trying to produce a Large Number of the same Product, while the sales people were using the Relationship-First Formula to develop Quality Relationships by delivering Unique Value.

Strategic fragmentation is further exacerbated by other players who have their own unique agenda. For example, the Information Technology department might be focused on implementing an advanced IT system, but the question is: "Are they building the system to meet the objectives of the engineering/manufacturing department, or the objectives of the sales/marketing department?" Or perhaps they have their own completely unique objectives. Obviously, if everyone is using different business models and going in different strategic directions, the company can't focus all its effort and resources on delivering Unique Value to its customers.

The high cost paid by a company with fragmented models, strategies and systems is always apparent to me when I conduct a Strategic System Audit. During the review, I have everyone in the company complete a Personal System Assessment that asks them to estimate how much time they spend (out of a total of 100 percent) on these three activities:

- Customer-Focused Activities (Delivering Unique Value)
- Capability Development (Creating Unique Value)
- Low-Value Activities (All other activities)

On average, respondents say they spend the following time on these activities:

- Customer-Focused Activities: (10 percent)
- Capability Development: (5 percent)
- Low-Value Activities: (85 percent)

This means that people in product-centric companies spend, on average, only 15 percent of their time creating or delivering Unique Value to their customers, or more bluntly, only 15 percent of their time making money. The rest of their time (85 percent) is wasted on low value activities such as filling out forms, fixing computer problems, finding things in filing cabinets, changing light bulbs, scheduling appointments, looking for information, retyping information, manipulating data, looking at web sites, meeting with accountants and lawyers, opening mail, reading e-mail, checking voice-mail, and paying bills: In other words, activities that don't make the company any money. Interestingly, when asked how much time they would like to spend on these activities, respondents answer on average:

- Customer-Focused Activities: (80 percent)
- Capability Development: (15 percent)
- Low-Value Activities: (5 percent)

These people want to spend 95 percent of their time creating and delivering Unique Value to their customers, and only five percent of their time on low-value activities—almost the exact opposite of their current situation! The question is: Why is there such a gap between their current situation and what they would like to be doing? The answer is: People in product-centric companies are prevented from creating and delivering Unique Value because their systems are fragmented, and their systems are fragmented because the people are not working together as a team. Therefore, you can only deliver Unique Value through Teamwork.

Why has Teamwork been such a failure in most organizations in spite of more than three decades of team workshops, team getaways, and team motivation exercises? I believe there are three reasons.

First, teamwork is not truly possible in any company designed around its products. In these organizations, there will always be a clash between the Product Hemisphere and the Customer Hemisphere. True teamwork is only possible if the strategic focus of the entire company is centered around customers.

Second, most companies still use an industrial top-down approach to planning and strategic decision-making. Presidents and managers still concoct their grand visions in isolation, and deliver orders to the troops. This dictatorial approach won't work because today's highly individualized troops will resist any plan they haven't helped create. More important, the plan probably won't work anyway because it was not designed using the key knowledge of the troops.

Third, teamwork programs fail because the company has not put into place what I call the Teamwork Capability. They don't build teams to develop detailed models for better strategies and systems. They don't work in teams to bring their fragmented systems together. They don't set out detailed step-by-step plans for achieving their visions. They don't ensure each individual team member takes action, on a regular, consistent basis, to achieve the vision. And most important, they don't invest time, money, and resources to develop better strategies and systems. (I will discuss how to implement the Team Work Capability in Chapter 7, "Your Strategic Transformation.")

When your company becomes a Relationship-First Enterprise, you will have the advanced structures, systems, methods and technology to make Teamwork a reality. Everyone will be focused on delivering Unique Value to your designated Customer Types. All of your company's systems will be integrated to deliver Unique Value. Everyone will use the same strategies and systems. Everyone will communicate the same core messages about the company. All of the company's marketing materials—brochures, websites, videos, advertising, news releases, presentations, packaging—will convey the same look and message. All of your company's key data information will be stored in a centralized database system accessible to everyone in the company. Everyone will understand the mission of the company, how the company is performing, and what is required to achieve further progress. Individual workers will take personal responsibility for what they need to do, and understand how their actions affect the overall organization.

How does the Relationship-First Enterprise achieve this kind of coordinated Teamwork? Once again, it all starts with the Relationship-First Formula. When a company provides Unique Value to a specific Customer Type, it's much easier for all the workers to understand their role, and how they can contribute. Specifically, the Relationship-First Enterprise has adopted the following team-building strategies:

- **Create a Relationship-First Leadership Team:** This team is comprised of representatives from each department of the company. You work together to create detailed models of the future, to formulate collective strategies, and to design unified, integrated systems to support your models and strategies.

- **Incorporate input from everyone:** In The Relationship-First Enterprise, everyone is involved, in some way, in developing the new vision. Your Leadership Team will get input from everyone in the company, and everyone's input will be considered. Instead of deploying a corporate vision from the top down, everyone will share in the development of the vision, and this means everyone will also buy into the changes and actions required to achieve the vision.

- **The vision and strategy are communicated clearly to everyone:** When your Leadership Team has devised new models, strategies, and systems, these decisions must be communicated clearly to everyone in the organization. Everyone should understand the vision and how it will be achieved.

- **Meet regularly to review vision and make key decisions:** Once you embark on the path of Teamwork, it is vital to consistently maintain the process. Your Leadership Team should meet consistently—every week, every two weeks, every month, quarterly, or every six months—to review your vision, celebrate your achievements, and make new strategic decisions.

The Three Key Concepts of Principal Strategy #3:
1. By helping to integrate all of your business systems and strategies, Teamwork enhances your ability to create and deliver Unique Value.
2. You will be better able to work together as a team if you use the Relationship-First Formula.
3. Form a Leadership Team to develop together model systems and strategies for your company.

Principal Strategy #4: Envision Ideal System Models

The Relationship-First Enterprise begins every project or initiative with a vision: a detailed blueprint of the ideal outcome. I call this vision the Ideal System Model. The model is designed to serve a clear purpose, and achieve specific objectives. It is based on fundamental principles and strategies that are independent of any technology, physical structure, or individual person.

For example, to create an e-marketing system, you start by designing the Ideal System Model for e-marketing. You determine the purpose of your system, the objectives to be achieved, the marketing strategy, the relationship-building process, and the specific communications functions you want the system to facilitate. You create the Ideal System Model without making reference to any particular technology or to any of your existing systems. Instead, you start with a clean slate. Only after you have completed the model do you seek out technology that will support it, and determine if any of your existing systems can be used (if not, they are eventually abandoned). In this way, you are not blinded or led astray by a particular kind of technology, or by the systems you already have in place.

As a Relationship-First Enterprise, you may need to design models for your overall business, your marketing programs, your value delivery system, your human and physical resources, and so on. There is, in fact, no end to the models you will create as you move forward into the future as a Relationship-First Enterprise. The key point is this: As such an enterprise, you will start all projects and initiatives with the

Ideal System Model. Before you proceed with any action, installation or investment, you will clearly define the Customer Type, your goals, the process, the principles, and your strategies.

The danger of proceeding without doing this has become apparent to me in working with more than 4,000 companies over the 25 years. I discovered that organizations take one of two approaches when they want to improve and grow their business: the Incremental Method, or the Ideal System Model. Using the Incremental Method, they make small step-by-step improvements to existing systems. They produce a more professional brochure. They hire more motivated salespeople. Or they add new software to their computers.

Each of these improvements—while beneficial in a small way—is just an add-on to existing systems, and if the basic structure of these systems is flawed, the incremental improvements have very little positive impact on the overall fortunes of the company. For example, they may have the best sales force in the world, but if the core business model is flawed, their business will fail unless they change the model. Or they may have a stunning website, but if their e-marketing model is flawed, their site will be a waste of time and money.

Unfortunately, most companies today use the incremental method, and try to succeed by patching up their fundamentally flawed systems. They do this for a number of reasons. Primarily, companies use this method because they spend most of their time living in the past. They can't envision an ideal model of the future because they have so much invested in what they have already done. They won't create an ideal database system, because they have spent millions on their existing, poorly designed system. They won't create a more effective website because they have spent three years building their existing one. Or they won't create a better marketing system because they have too much invested in their existing marketing tools and programs, even though they don't work. They won't think about an ideal future because they're shackled with legacy investments, entrenched bureaucracies, and office politics.

Companies use the ineffective incremental method because they don't have the courage to make the changes necessary to implement an ideal system. They would rather suffer than work towards a much more desirable future.

And finally, most companies use this method because it has been used for more than 200 years since the start of the Industrial Revolution. Like the Product-First Formula, the incremental method is ingrained in our culture. Most of us don't know any other way to shape our future. But in our age of accelerating change, we can't use the past as a road map. We have to constantly look forward. We have to decide what kind of future we want, and move progressively towards that ideal.

Companies also use the incremental method because they have *Technopia*. This means they build their systems by starting with a specific kind of technology. For example, if they want to build a database system, they purchase database software first and build their system around it. If they discover later that the database software can't do something they want, they either make compromises, or they try to add on another program. Eventually, they end up with a horrendous monstrosity that doesn't achieve their objectives, and costs a fortune to build. Technopia, which afflicts most companies, is not limited to computer-related systems. Companies exhibit the symptoms of Technopia when they build their business systems around an office building, or a particular person, or a specific kind of marketing tool. They don't succeed because they start their thinking with a specific tool.

As an illustration, let's look at a company called EGO Unlimited that has been stuck at the Performance Plateau because it continues to use the incremental method. EGO Unlimited is a leading supplier of industrial flange capacitors for the electrical utility sector. The company wants to grow its business by entering new markets, and by introducing new products, but its growth has been stalled for more than three years. Every time the company tried to grow—by adding new salespeople and by launching new marketing programs—its business systems were unable to cope with the added complexity. When the company doubled its salespeople, its sales information system couldn't cope with the increase in communications traffic. When it expanded its advertising and direct mail programs, the marketing department couldn't cope with the increase in demand for product literature. When it introduced new products, its warehouse couldn't cope with the increase in orders.

EGO Unlimited experiences these problems because it takes action before designing Ideal System Models. It tries to create and deliver more value by making incremental changes to its existing systems. Unfortunately, the existing systems—designed for a much smaller organization—are unable to keep up with the company's goals and objectives. Rather than simply expanding what it already has, the company needs to create and build Ideal System Models first before adding salespeople, products, and marketing programs.

Fortunately, making the switch from the incremental method to the Ideal System Model is quite easy. Just start each project by thinking about the ideal system. Think first: "What do I really want to achieve? What is the purpose of this system? What process will this system support? What would the ideal system look like?" Working with your team, make detailed drawings of the Ideal System Model. Describe it thoroughly. Determine the actions required to build the ideal system. Ask yourself: "What technology will be needed to support the model? What parts of our existing system will we use to build the ideal system? What parts of our existing system do we need to scrap? What new people and resources will we need to invest in?

Of course, in the real world, achieving your ideal is not always possible right away. Your vision of the ideal model will be constantly changing as you move forward and grow. As well, it might not be possible to dump your existing systems in the short-term. For political or economic reasons, you might have to make do with what you have for the time being. But these realities do not eclipse the value of starting all action with the Ideal System Model. With this model in place, you can begin immediately to move closer to the ideal. Every action you take will be guided by your vision of the ideal future. When you have the time, money, or resources to make progress towards the ideal, you will know what to do. You won't drift off course. Your ideal will serve as your lighthouse. It might take you longer than you want to reach shore, but you will always be steering in the right direction.

In Chapter 7, "Your Strategic Transformation," I explain in detail how to design and implement Ideal System Models.

The Three Key Concepts of Principal Strategy #4:
1. Before you take action, begin every project or initiative by envisioning the Ideal System Model.
2. Significant progress is not possible if you try to make incremental improvements to existing systems that are fundamentally flawed.
3. By starting with The Ideal System Model, you can move towards your ideal system at your own pace, depending on your available time, money, and resources.

Principal Strategy #5:
Give Away Value to Start Quality Relationships

As we discussed in Chapter 2, "The Global Reality," prospects are harder to reach in today's global economy. Bombarded by sales messages, most consumers today have a serious case of sensory overload. They just don't want to hear another sales pitch, so they hide behind technology such as voice-mail and call-display. They have assistants screen their calls, and, when watching TV, they block out commercials with their remote control. They do just about anything to avoid salespeople hawking products and services.

To succeed in this anti-sales environment, the Relationship-First Enterprise abandons the traditional hard-sell approach of the Industrial Age. Instead of trying to "sell" to prospects, The Relationship First Enterprise "attracts" prospects by giving them something of value to start the relationship. I call this approach Attractor Marketing.

Like all the principal strategies, Attractor Marketing is a philosophy that permeates the Relationship-First Enterprise. At every turn, the Relationship-First Enterprise provides value before it expects to receive anything in return. Its salespeople give seminars, not sales presentations. Its website contains valuable content, not just brochure copy and catalogue listings. Its stores provide an exciting experience, not just a place to buy things. All of these strategies are designed to attract prospects of their own free will to the company.

For example, let's say you're a salesperson for EGO Unlimited. For the past five years, you've made sales presentations to prospects, but each year you notice prospects are harder and harder to reach. When you make cold calls, you hardly ever get through. You get voicemail or an assistant. If you do speak with your prospect, they say they're too busy to meet with you, or they make up some excuse. No matter what you do, no one wants to hear your sales pitch about industrial flange capacitors.

So what do you do? How do you get through to prospects in the electrical utility sector? The answer is: Give Away Value to Start Relationships! Instead of making a sales presentation, tell prospects you will do a free survey of their electrical facility. Invite them to a seminar about electrical management. Provide them with a library of articles. Give them an educational video, or a database, or private access to a members-only website. Each of these initiatives will attract the attention of your prospects, and they will come to you to receive the free value. In doing so, you will have a chance to introduce yourself and begin your business relationship.

To illuminate more fully the concept of Attractor Marketing, let's consider websites. Most websites fail because they're only electronic brochures. They're a digital sales pitch. In the e-marketing environment, which is essentially non-intrusive, people will not visit a website unless they have a reason to do so. A sales-pitch website about a company's products, its staff, and the size of its factories is boring. It doesn't offer prospective customers any value, so they have no inclination to visit it. A website based on the principles of Attractor Marketing, however, is much more effective. If the site provides prospects with an incredible amount of free value—important non-partisan information, useful databases, expert advice, powerful software, or entertaining content—they will be attracted to it.

The Relationship-First Enterprise always provides free value during the sales and marketing process, but it can also go a lot further. It can create revenue-generating marketing tools such as high-quality books, videos, seminars, CD-ROMs, and online services. The Relationship-First Enterprise can transform its marketing function from an expense into a source of revenue. I call this Revenue Marketing. For example, this book is a Revenue Marketing project for my company. People pay for it, and it helps me market my other products and services. I make money from this marketing tool because I spent more than a year creating its value.

So the key point is: If you want to attract prospects, and even make money from your marketing efforts, you have to add a higher level of value to your marketing programs. Instead of seeing marketing as an expense, you have to look at it as an investment and as a potential source of revenue. To attract the right prospects, you need to develop a Controlling Promotional Idea (CPI) for each of your designated Customer Types (CT). This is a universal promotional concept that clearly defines the free value you are willing to provide in order to start a new relationship. For example, at EGO Unlimited, the company has developed a Controlling Promotional Idea called the Flange Efficiency Program. The program offers electrical utility managers a free efficiency test for their flange capacitors. Prospects can also download free flange efficiency software from the EGO Unlimited website and access a free database of articles on flange capacitor mechanics. All of this free value is designed to attract electrical utility managers so EGO Unlimited can begin relationships with them. I will discuss the Controlling Promotional Idea in more detail in Chapter 7, "Your Strategic Transformation."

The Three Key Concepts of Principal Strategy #5:
1. Because prospects are harder and harder to reach, you must "attract" them to your company of their own free will.
2. To attract prospects, you must provide "free" value before you make a sales pitch.
3. The free value must provide an obvious no-strings-attached benefit to the prospect. This value is defined by the Controlling Promotional Idea.

Principal Strategy #6:
Offer Components of Unique Value

In Chapter 1, we looked at a company called Trinity Gear & Rod. As you may recall, the company had trouble keeping up with customer demands for made-to-order, just-in-time gears and rods. Their information, manufacturing, and distribution systems were not designed to serve the unique needs of each individual customer. Their systems were designed around their products, not around their customers. As such, they lost customers, and missed out on many potentially profitable opportunities.

The lesson to be learned from Trinity Gear & Rod and from hundreds of other product-first companies is clear. To thrive in today's fast-paced marketplace, you must quickly seize profitable and unforeseen opportunities as they arise. You must rapidly assemble your Unique Value in new ways to meet the individual needs of potential customers. All of your systems and strategies must support rapid customization. Every asset of your organization—products, services, information, knowledge, and human resources—must be broken down into its fundamental component parts. Your database systems must allow you to put these components together quickly, or ideally, give your customers the ability to assemble the components themselves.

That's why the Relationship-First Enterprise offers components of Unique Value or Value Components (VC). Instead of building its systems and strategies around specific products or services, The Relationship-First Enterprise develops a continuous supply of Value Components which can be assembled in an infinite variety of combinations. In this way, these components allow the Relationship-First Enterprise to thrive in an age of accelerating change, increasing competition, and instant communication.

To illustrate the concept of Value Components, let's pretend you run a textbook company called Ivory Tower Publishing. In the past, you published more than 5,000 textbooks worldwide. You also had lots of competition, and you were caught in the Commodity Trap. There wasn't much to distinguish you or your products from the hundreds of other textbook publishers. However, when you learned about Value Components, you realized your text books were actually composed of more than 100,000 different components—chapters, articles, case studies, research notes, and analyses. You created a database of these components and their content. Your customers—students and academics—can now build their own unique text books by assembling these components. The customized, one-of-a-kind text books can be created and downloaded online in single editions, or in the case of large orders, printed. In this way, Ivory Tower Publishing can now deliver Unique Value to each individual customer. The company makes a higher profit because it doesn't have to pre-print books or carry inventory. The company can also charge more for its textbooks because each one is a custom order. As well, Ivory Tower only pays the component providers (writers, researchers, teachers), when their component is purchased by a customer.

By switching from a business model based on specific products (text books) to a model based on Value Components (components of information), Ivory Tower Publishing now thrives because of accelerating change, increasing competition, and instant communication. The company now welcomes change because its customers are always looking for new information. The company no longer has any comparable competition because everyone else sells specific textbooks. In fact, many of its competitors have become suppliers. They supply Ivory Tower with the raw material for its Value Components. As well, instant communication technology such as e-mail and the web have made it possible for Ivory Tower to deliver its Value Components inexpensively to a worldwide audience. In other words, Ivory Tower thrives because of the Global Reality.

In addition to products and services, the concept of Value Components is applied to every system and strategy of the Relationship-First Enterprise. For example, its marketing material is divided into components. Instead of printing a brochure—which will go out of date in a few days or months—the Relationship-First Enterprise creates unique brochures from components of its marketing material. When customers ask for information about the company, the Relationship-First Enterprise can quickly send each person a customized promotional package which meets their unique needs and requests.

As another example, this kind of enterprise creates a database listing the skills and knowledge of each individual employee. Each skill is considered a separate Value Component. When the company wants to accomplish a specific project, it determines the required group of skills. The project team is assembled by bringing together people who possess the required skill components.

A third example is filing and organizational systems. Every item of information—either in print or digital form—is stored in its component parts. For instance, suppose you want to create a library of more than 2,000 photographs. You use a database to record and file each photograph by number as a separate component. When you want to put together a group of these photographs, you use the database to quickly search for and assemble them.

Managed by databases, component-based systems and strategies offer many advantages. They give you the flexibility to deliver custom products and services, and allow you to respond quickly to profitable, unforeseen opportunities. Properly designed, component-based systems are also infinitely expandable—you can add an endless number of new Value Components. Component-based systems also give you the ability to serve the unique needs of specific Customer Types and add new Customer Types more easily. As well, because component-based systems are so efficient, you have more time to spend on Customer-Focused Activities (Delivering Value) and Capability Development (Creating Value).

The Three Key Concepts of Principal Strategy #6:
1. To thrive in an age of accelerating change, you must offer components of Unique Value or Value Components, instead of specific products or services.
2. By offering Value Components, you can better meet the unique needs of your customers and prospects, and seize profitable, unforeseen opportunities as they arise.

3. The concept of Value Components should be applied to every system and strategy used by the Relationship-First Enterprise.

Principal Strategy #7: Develop a Mass Customization Planning Process

To help its customers choose the right Value Components, the Relationship-First Enterprise walks them through a Mass Customization Planning Process. This process allows the prospect/customer to assess their current situation, establish clear goals, make a plan, and then choose the right tools to implement the plan. In this way, every customer goes through exactly the same process and yet ends up with a unique, customized solution.

Companies using The Product-First Model do not facilitate this kind of mass customization. Their manufacturing and delivery process is set up to deliver large numbers of the same product/service. This one-size-fits-all approach might be efficient for the company, but it leaves most customers feeling unsatisfied.

Faced with customer demands for customized solutions, the Product-First company is thrown into turmoil because its systems are not designed to deal with custom orders. They either refuse, or provide the custom solution at a loss. The trick is to provide a customized solution in an efficient manner. This is the objective of mass customization; the best of both worlds.

A mass customization system is designed along the spine of a decision line. This is a series of steps, each step being the selection of options. To visualize this concept, imagine a mass customization automobile factory. The factory is set up to give each person a customized car in an efficient and profitable manner.

At step one, the customer chooses from a variety of car types (sports car, van, SUV, pickup truck). At step two, the customer chooses from 18 different types of wheels. At step three, they choose the color of the car. At step four, they choose from 10 different kinds of steering wheels.

And so on. At the end of the line, the car pops out exactly the way the customer wanted it. And right behind it, five minutes later, another car pops out exactly the way that customer wanted it.

The key insight here is: Every customer went through exactly the same step-by-step process, and yet every customer got a unique solution. Another key element of this approach is that the process is designed to help the customer make choices at each step. They are an active participant in the selection process.

By setting up this kind of mass customization process, the Relationship-First Enterprise is able to provide Unique Value in a profitable manner. It is also able to adapt instantly to changes in technology and market preferences. For example, if people stop buying SUVs and started buying more sports car, the auto company would be able to meet this change in demand without retooling its factory because its system was set up in the first place to handle accelerating change.

In most case, you will not be selling products such as cars or tennis shoes. You will be selling something intangible. This makes it even more important to set up a mass customization system in your company. In this case, your process involves the five steps mentioned previously. They are a universal process that can be used in any business, both tangible and intangible.

The steps of the process are:
1. Assess current situation
2. Establish goals
3. Create plan
4. Choose tools
5. Implement plan

Step 1: Assess current situation: In the first step, you help your prospect/customer assess their current situation. They determine what is working for them, and what isn't working. Then they tell you what they think they need to do to improve their situation. This step can be facilitated through verbal questioning, written questionnaires and scorecards.

Step 2: Establish goals: It is hard for you to help your customers if you don't know their goals. It is even harder for you to help them if they don't know what their goals are. That's why this step is so important. To provide the right solutions, you and your customers need to have a written statement of their goals. It seems obvious, but this step is rarely done in a Product-First situation because the product seller doesn't want to find out that the product they are pushing won't help the customer achieve their goals. However, a Relationship-First Enterprise always wants to know what their customers goals are.

Step 3: Create a plan: It is important to stress that it is the customer who makes the plan, not the supplier. In a product-first environment, the company will often go away and return with a plan for the customer to consider. But this usually doesn't work because there is usually little buy-in from the customer. Obversely, the Relationship-First Enterprise helps the customer make their own plan by asking them a series of questions. As a result, there is total buy-in from the customer because they made their own plan.

Step 4: Choose tools: At this point, the customer is ready to choose from a toolbox of products and services. They are given a complete list of the available resources, and assisted in the selection process. These tools are both internal to the company, and external, provided through experts who are strategic partners. This is markedly contrasted to a product-first situation where the company only offers the limited number of products/services that they provide directly.

It is also important to state at this point that step 4 is the pay off for the Relationship-First Enterprise. By providing a vast selection of every possible Value Component, the Relationship-First Enterprise has the opportunity to sell a much larger number of products and services. This seems ironic, but is true. The company that focuses first on products will sell less products, and the company that focuses first on relationships will sell a lot more products.

Step 5: Implement the plan: Once the plan has been made and the tools selected, the Relationship-First Enterprise now helps the customer implement their plan. This can involved months or years of activity. The key is that the Relationship-First Enterprise acts at the overall facilitator or contractor for the implementation, overseeing the work of both internal and external workers. In this way, the Relationship-First Enterprise maintains its core role in the relationship with the customer, in fact, still owing the relationship with the customer. It is also able to turn former competitors into revenue sources by incorporating their products and services into their toolbox.

By walking its customers through this five-step process, the Relationship-First Enterprise achieves its full potential by providing Unique Value and Quality Relationships. It is also set up to take full advantage of the global realities of accelerating change, increasing competition, and instant communication.

Principal Strategy #8: Develop Capabilities, not Tools

Most companies never overcome the Performance Plateau because they invest most of their time, effort, and money developing tools instead of capabilities. For example, let's say you hire a graphic designer to produce a new company brochure for a "retailers" trade show. The brochure looks great, and it's a big hit with the retailers at the show. Six months later, however, you have a problem. You have to get ready for another trade show, this time for "distributors." But your retailer brochure won't work for the distributors. As well, a lot of the content in the retailer brochure is now out of date. In six months, you've added 10 new products, and opened three new locations. To produce a new "distributors" brochure, you call the graphic designer, but she is no longer available. You realize you're back to square one. You have to produce a new brochure from scratch. You have this problem because you developed a tool (a brochure) instead of a capability (the ability to produce custom brochures quickly and easily).

But look at the Relationship-First Enterprise. To get ready for the same "retailer" trade show, it took a much difference approach. Instead of creating a tool, it decided to develop a capability: A value components database of its 300 products and services. The database project took more time, effort and money than it would have taken to produce a brochure, but the superior benefits of the new system were immediately apparent. To prepare for the retail trade show, the marketing manager used the database to generate a custom retail brochure by selecting the retail products list. Six months later, the marketing manager created a distributors brochure by selecting the distributors product list. As well, other people in the company began using the value components database in hundreds of different ways. Sales used it to prepare custom packages for presentations. Engineering used it to record and access product specifications. Finance used it to build price lists and invoices. And Distribution used it to build inventory records. As well, Marketing realized they could use the database as an online catalogue on the website.

As you can see, by investing in a capability, the Relationship-First Enterprise was able to realize tremendous gains in productivity and flexibility. If a new opportunity arises, the value components database gives them the ability to put forward a unique solution quickly and professionally. Although the value components database cost more initially to create than a brochure, the capability paid for itself in a matter of months; now the company never has to create new brochures from scratch.

To illuminate this principal strategy, it's instructive to define tools and capabilities more clearly. Tools provide a short-term benefit or an immediate solution to specific problems for a small, finite number of people. Tools are usually created in isolation by one person or by a single department and cannot be readily employed by other people or departments. Tools are suitable only for specific purposes and have a limited life span. As such, the return is extremely low on the time, money and effort invested in developing a tool.

For example, at EGO Unlimited, Beatrice in Marketing has spent five years building a database for distributing their newsletter, The EGO Report. She has amassed more 25,000 names using a database program called The Newsletter Peoplizer. Beatrice loves her database, but she's the only one who uses it. In the direct marketing department, Horace has his own database with more than 200,000 names. He uses a program called DirectFinder. Meanwhile, down in Finance, Perry uses BookSoft for keeping track of customer accounts.

Beatrice, Horace, and Perry may have increased their personal productivity by using their own software programs, but there is one big problem. By focusing on tools, EGO Unlimited doesn't have the capability to share information between departments. Data can't be pulled together quickly, or in innovative ways. Responding to new, unforeseen opportunities is difficult. As well, Beatrice, Horace and Perry are limited. The Newsletter Peoplizer helps Beatrice with newsletters, but it doesn't help her manage sales conferences, and client presentations. For these tasks, she has to use other software programs. To pull together a project, she spends a lot of time transferring information from one kind of database to another. It is extremely inefficient. So, Beatrice spends a lot of time on low-value activities—finding, processing, and distributing information—and very little time creating and delivering value to customers.

Capabilities, on the other hand, provide long-term benefits and far-reaching solutions for everyone associated with the company. Capabilities are created by teams, not individuals. They are company-wide systems designed with a long-term perspective. Capabilities help the Relationship-First Enterprise seize new, unforeseen opportunities. Capabilities are an investment in the future, not just the present. Capabilities also free the Relationship-First Enterprise from the Performance Plateau. By increasing efficiency and flexibility in all areas of its business, capabilities increase the amount of time the Relationship-First Enterprise spends on creating and delivering value, and decreases the amount of time it spends on low-value activities. It also frees up time to spend on developing further capabilities, which in turn increases its ability to create and deliver value. This upward spiral, based on the concept of capabilities instead of tools, ensures that The Relationship-First Enterprise enjoys much greater growth and success than a company that keeps creating tools over and over again.

Here are a few examples of how you can develop capabilities, not tools, in specific areas of your business.

Strategic Planning: Instead of developing tactics to deal with specific issues (tools), develop long-term models and strategies that give your company the ability to deal with issues quickly and efficiently as they arise (capability).

Manufacturing: Instead of buying a machine that makes a specific part (tool), buy a machine that can be quickly retooled to make millions of different parts (capability).

Software: Instead of using software that performs a specific function (tool), use "building-block" software that allows you to create your own custom programs and software solutions (capability).

Marketing Materials: Instead of creating specific marketing materials such as a brochure (tool), develop systems that allow you to create custom brochures quickly and easily (capability).

Office organization: Instead of cleaning up the mess in your office every month (tool), develop organization systems that keep your office neat and tidy all the time.

Staff: Instead of always looking for new people for specific jobs (tools), develop systems that enable you to source and hire talented workers when the need arises (capability).

Teams: Instead of setting up teams for specific projects (tool), develop systems that allow you to set up teams quickly, and allow them to work together efficiently and effectively (capability).

Training and Education: Instead of teaching employees how to do a specific task (tool), teach them the underlying principles and concepts so they can innovate and do it themselves when new tasks need to be done (capability)

Although most people know capabilities are superior to tools, there are many reasons why most companies focus almost exclusively on tools. First, they don't want to spend the extra money to develop capabilities. They only have a short-term financial perspective. Second, they don't take the time out of their day-to-day activities to build better systems. They are just too time-stressed. They have too many things on their plate. But ironically, by making and using tools, they never get out of their bind. They are always too busy to make their system better. Third, they just don't understand the concept of capabilities. They don't even think about making their systems better. It's not on their agenda. As such, they are doomed forever to languish on the Performance Plateau.

The concept of capabilities vs. tools also applies to business models and strategies. Often a company is too busy or too short-sighted to invest in better business models or more effective strategies. The company's leaders would rather continue using an outdated business model that doesn't work than spend some time developing a new business model. Or they continue to use ineffective strategies because they don't want to stop taking action on a day-to-day basis. As well, they don't put in place systems that help them to constantly assess their business models and strategies. Once again, this focus on specific models and strategies (tools), traps a company on the Performance Plateau.

To become a Relationship-First Enterprise, your company must start to develop better capabilities. You have to take the time, and invest the money, to plan and build better systems. In Chapter 7, "Your Strategic Transformation," I will explain how to plan and build new capabilities in your company.

The Three Key Concepts of Principal Strategy #8:

1. A tool provides a short-term benefit or an immediate solution to a specific problem for a small, finite number of people.
2. A capability provides long-term benefits and far-reaching solutions for everyone associated with your organization.
3. By developing capabilities, not tools, you increase the amount of time your company can spend creating and delivering value to your customers.

Principal Strategy #9: Ride The Strategic Dip

Companies and individuals are often stranded at the Performance Plateau because they're unwilling to experience any short-term decline in sales or productivity in order to achieve a bigger result in the future. They are simply unwilling to go down before going up. I call this Riding The Strategic Dip.

For example, let's say your company has been marketing educational products and services to high school teachers for more than two decades. Sales in recent years have gone flat, but you still make a modest profit. Research shows you could expand your business dramatically by adapting your products for parents who want to teach their children themselves, but you realize you would have to invest a lot of money, and a lot of time, to create the new products, and promote them to the new market. As well, you would have to pull resources out of the high school market, and suffer a one-year decline in overall sales revenue. Although you have made an excellent case for pursuing the parent market, your investors will not tolerate a decline in revenue and dividends. Senior management is also afraid they'll lose their jobs if revenues take a decline, even if it is only temporary. So the new marketing project is shelved, and you continue selling text books to school teachers. Any prospect of a bigger, brighter future is unlikely because your company is unwilling to go down before going up.

Sadly, most companies—big and small—take this approach. They have simply stopped taking risks and have stopped growing as a result. This is ironic because most companies were started by entrepreneurs willing to go down before going up. The entrepreneurs may have quit a job, or a made a large investment, in order to start the company. Initially, they probably made very little money, but eventually the investment paid off. By going down before going up, they realized a bigger, brighter future. Unfortunately, the entrepreneurs, or the people who succeeded them, stopped taking risks at some point. They reached a certain level of prosperity and comfort, and they were unwilling to get uncomfortable again. So they languished at the Performance Plateau.

The Relationship-First Enterprise, on the other hand, takes a totally different approach. For example, when the company decides to pursue a new Customer Type by creating new Unique Value, it prepares to ride The Strategic Dip. Everyone involved with the company—employees, senior management, investors, bankers, suppliers and customers—understands they must go down before they go up. When sales revenue drops temporarily for six months, everyone knows the organization has just stopped delivering value so it can spend some time creating value. There is no panic. The Strategic Dip is a planned event, executed for a good reason, to realize a bigger, long-term goal. In this way, the Relationship-First Enterprise continues to grow bigger and better by taking a series of planned dips, followed by a period of dramatic growth.

To become a Relationship-First Enterprise, your company must incorporate this strategy into its culture. Everyone must be willing, and allowed, to go down before going up. For example, if your office is disorganized, you must take time out to organize it better. If you do, you will be able to deliver a lot more value in the future. Or perhaps your marketing programs aren't working. You need to stop executing the programs, and plan better ones. The short-term loss in sales will pay off in greater sales in the future. Or maybe your computer systems are inefficient. You need to stop using them and create better systems. By taking time out, you will be much more efficient in the long run. The lesson here is simple. In each of these cases, a long-term benefit was realized because you were willing to go down before going up.

The concept of The Strategic Dip will help you implement this strategy. If you or your company needs to regroup, reorganize, or retool, simply plan and execute a Strategic Dip. Plan ahead and schedule it. Put aside money to pay for it. Communicate your intentions and state the goal of your temporary pause in upward growth. By taking a series of planned downturns you will develop the ability to constantly grow your business by making it better and better.

The Three Key Concepts of Principal Strategy #9:
1. To realize a bigger, brighter future, you may have to go down before going up.
2. Companies willing to experience short-term declines in revenue and

productivity in order to create new Unique Value are mostly likely to realize the highest levels of future growth.

3. To get support for a temporary decline from investors, senior management, employees and other people related to your company, you need to plan, prepare for, and execute a Strategic Dip.

The Strategy of Strategies

If you adopt the nine Principal Strategies presented in this chapter, your company will have an excellent chance to thrive in the 21st century. The Principal Strategies will help you replace the outmoded Product-First Formula with the new Relationship-First Formula. The strategies will help you deal with the Post-Product Reality, and overcome the Performance Plateau by addressing your Limiting Factors.

But most significantly, they will also help you develop an important capability of the Relationship-First Enterprise: the capacity to identify and take charge of the strategies ingrained in the culture of your company. I call this ability the Strategy of Strategies.

By learning and adopting the nine Principal Strategies, you and your team will start operating at a much higher strategic level: at the level of concepts, symbols, principles, and paradigms. You will be able to identify and discard old strategies (such as the Product-First Formula) that are hurting your business. You will be able to develop new, positive strategies that will propel your business forward. You will be able to identify and address the deep psychological and cultural influences that have taken hold in your company. You will be able to create and employ your own principal strategies. You will have become a Relationship-First Enterprise.

In the next chapter, "The Relationship-First Enterprise," I give you a detailed description of a company built around the Relationship-First Formula.

CHAPTER 5:
The Relationship-First Enterprise

> *"Efficiency of a practically flawless kind may be reached naturally in the struggle for bread. But there is something beyond—a higher point, a subtle and unmistakable touch of love and pride beyond mere skill; almost an inspiration which gives to all work that finish which is almost art—which is art."*
>
> **Joseph Conrad: *The Mirror of the Sea***

Transforming your company into a Relationship-First Enterprise is more than just a quest for money, or for greater productivity. It's a quest for a "higher point", something beyond "the struggle for bread." In Joseph Conrad's words, it's a mission to build something that is "almost an inspiration which gives to all work that finish which is almost art—which is art."

As a work of art, the Relationship-First Enterprise represents an ideal: the archetype of the perfect company, an organization that thrives within the 21st century environment of accelerating change, increasing competition, and instant communication. Like all ideal models, of course, the Relationship-First Enterprise also represents an unattainable state of perfection. No one has created the perfect company, and no one ever will. However, the Relationship-First Enterprise gives you an ideal or model to aspire to. It will motivate and guide you as you plan, build, and transform your business in the 21st century.

Here then, are the model characteristics of the Relationship-First Enterprise.

Business Model Based On the Relationship-First Formula

The Relationship-First Enterprise has accepted the fact that we live in a revved-up world. It acknowledges that the old business models, which had their genesis during the Industrial Revolution, no longer work in the 21st century. As such, the Relationship-First Enterprise has abandoned the Product-First Formula, (Product x Large Number = Success), and has adopted the Relationship-First Formula (Quality Relationships x Unique Value = Success.) The goal of the Relationship-First Enterprise is to develop Quality Relationships by providing Unique Value to a specific type of customer. As such, all of its strategies, systems, capabilities, and marketing programs are designed around its customers, not around its products or services.

Strategy Starts With Customer Type

The first strategic decision of the Relationship-First Enterprise is to select its Customer Type. The Relationship-First Enterprise selects its Customer Type based on many factors, including its experience, its existing expertise and capabilities, the competitive environment, and the market potential. The key point is, the Relationship-First Enterprise chooses its Customer Type, not its products or services, first.

For example, the company may choose *dog owners* as its Customer Type or *company presidents*, or *farmers*. Or it may choose more specialized Customer Types such as *bulldog owners*, or *presidents of software companies*, or *emu farmers*. In fact, the Relationship-First Enterprise may choose a promising Customer Type for which it does not currently have any existing products or services.

Note: The Relationship-First Enterprise can have more than one Customer Type, but it must deal with each type separately, even to the point of creating a separate company for each type. Note: However it must be noted that the most successful companies in the future will have only one Customer Type, which simplifies their operations, and makes them undisputed specialists and experts in their Customer Type category.

Unique Value Divided Into Components

When The Relationship-First Enterprise has selected its Customer Type, it develops components of Unique Value. These components are the smallest possible sub-units of products, services, and information that research and experience has shown will be of interest to its Customer Type. These components will be assembled by the company, or by the customer directly, into customized, individualized products or services. For example, a company with *recreational sailors* as its Customer Type will develop components of products (parts of sailboats), services (different kinds of boat charter services) and information (a database of information about sailing). Its customers, *recreational sailors*, can assemble these components into unique, customized sailboats, charter vacations, and sailing books. In this way, the Relationship-First Enterprise can continually improve the quality of its relationships with people who match its Customer Type by constantly adding new Value Components that will interest them.

Note: The Relationship-First Enterprise does not need to be the manufacturer of these Value Components. The company can employ the Value Components offered by other manufacturers, strategic partners, and even its competitors. In fact, the ideal Relationship-First Enterprise does not produce or deliver any of its Value Components. It merely acts as a gateway for products and services provided by other companies.

Capabilities Developed to Assemble Value Components

While the Relationship-First Enterprise accumulates its toolbox of Value Components, it also develops systems that facilitate the quick

assembly of these components by its employees, and possibly by its customers directly. These systems employ:
- databases that support the concept of Value Components;
- component-based filing systems (both physical and digital), supported by databases;
- capabilities that allow staff and customers to communicate in an integrated fashion over the telephone, e-mail, the Web, fax, in print; and
- facilities and equipment supporting the rapid manufacture and distribution of customized products and services.
- relationship-building activities that build partnerships with providers of Value Components.

All of the company's systems are designed around the customer, not around products, or specific types of technology. For example, its database or Information Technology (IT) system is designed around its People Database, not around its manufacturing, engineering, or financial databases. In this way, the systems reflect the Relationship-First Formula, not the outmoded Product-First Formula.

Free Value Given to Start Relationships

The Relationship-First Enterprise acknowledges that prospects are harder to reach in the 21st century. It knows hard-sell promotions, pitched through mediums such as advertising and commercial-laden websites, do not attract the kinds of prospects its wants. As such, to attract quality prospects that match its Customer Type, this enterprise gives away value at the start of relationships. Instead of jumping right to the sales pitch, the Relationship-First Enterprise offers prospects something valuable in exchange for the opportunity to begin the relationship.

For example, this kind of organization may offer prospects free products or services such as advice, seminars, books, software, or some kind of unique experience. In this way, The Relationship-First Enterprise breaks through the barriers set up by today's busy, sensory-overloaded consumer. Instead of selling, selling, selling, the Relationship-First

Enterprise attracts quality prospects of their own free will, either in person, over the telephone, on the Web, or through other marketing channels or technology.

The key point is: the Relationship-First Enterprise does not dynamically assault prospects with promotions, it attracts them by providing something valuable for free.

Marketing Program Created Around Customer Type

The Relationship-First Enterprise creates a marketing program designed around its Customer Type, not around its products and services. The program attracts the designated Customer Type by communicating clearly the free value and the Value Components provided by the company.

For example, let's assume a Relationship-First Enterprise has *brain surgeons* as its Customer Type. To serve this market, the company might create the Brain Surgeon Knowledge Program. The program is designed to provide an ever-increasing stream of Unique Value to *brain surgeons*. To initially attract *surgeons* to the program, The Relationship-First Enterprise gives them free access to other *brain surgeons* on its website. Once the *brain surgeons* have started using the website, the Relationship-First Enterprise makes money by providing them with thousands of other Value Components such as conferences, medical journals, books, equipment, and software.

Note: The marketing program is future-proof because it is independent of any marketing tool or technology. In addition to the Web, the company can also deliver *The Brain Surgeon Knowledge Program* through print material (magazines, newsletters, catalogues), over the telephone (1-900 services), by e-mail (e-newsletters), through multimedia (audio, video, CD-ROM/DVD), and in person at conferences and trade shows. It can also use any new tool or technology that comes along without changing the basic premise of the program itself. Note: Since the first edition of this book, new marketing technology such as social media have come on stream, becoming another marketing tool for the Relationship-First Enterprise.

Quality Relationships Fostered Using Centralized Database System

Databases are the brain of the Relationship-First Enterprise, and information about its prospects/customers is stored at the centre of this brain. Whenever the prospect/customer comes into contact with the Relationship-First Enterprise —in person, over the telephone, on the Web, through e-mail—information about the contact event is recorded in the database. All of the information can be combined, sorted, and analyzed. To facilitate this high degree of seamless data-gathering and analysis, this kind of enterprise operates an integrated, centralized database system designed around its customers. In this way, the Relationship-First Enterprise uses its database system to manage its relationships by using the information stored in it to plan and create new Unique Value for its customers.

Note: The issue of privacy arises when you start to collect information in your database. It is a complex issue, but one factor will likely keep you on the right track. If your customers feel you protect their privacy and safeguard the information you collect about them, they will continue to give you the information you need. If you don't respect their privacy, they will stop giving you the information you need.

Note: Since the first edition of this book, privacy concerns have escalated, especially regarding the use of private data by ISPs and social media sites.

Communicate on Mass, Individualized Basis

The Relationship-First Enterprise uses the information in its database system, and a host of tools and technology, to communicate with its customers on a mass, but individualized basis. The Relationship-First Enterprise has the capability to send all of its specific customers an e-mail, or printed letter, that offers each person a unique package of Value Components based on their individual interests, needs, or profile. This capability, often called Mass Customization, allows the Relationship-First Enterprise to develop even closer relationships with its customers.

For example, let's pretend a Relationship-First Enterprise has chosen *art collectors* as its Customer Type. To serve this market, the company has created The Art Collectors Global Network. The purpose of the program is to provide Art Collectors with a pantheon of Value Components including online auctions, art history seminars, art travel and tours, security services, and much, much more.

As each *art collector* comes into contact with the Relationship-First Enterprise, information is gathered about the individual (through conversations, interviews, surveys, and other automated methods) and then stored in the company's central database. By analyzing the data, the company can discern certain individual preferences for each person.

You might find through this process that Person A is interested mostly in Flemish Art. Person B is enamored of Classical Art, and Person C is a follower of Cubism. To cater to each person's unique interests, the company has developed the capability to automatically assemble and communicate information about the specific Value Components of interest to each person. As such, Person A receives information and promotions about Flemish Art, Person B about Classical Art, and Person C about Cubism.

In this way, the Relationship-First Enterprise is able to give individuals what they want, and only what they want. This type of mass, individualized communication further strengthens the Quality Relationships the Relationship-First Enterprise has with people who match its Customer Type.

Organizational Structure Based on the Relationship-First Formula

In a Product-First Company, the company focused on the creation and distribution of products. This product-first focus determined the organizational structure of the company. Traditionally, these departments are:
- research and development;
- manufacturing;
- sales and marketing;
- distribution; and
- finance

The Relationship-First Organizational Model has four departments:
- Relationship Management
- Value Creation and Delivery
- Ideas and Innovation Development
- Strategy and Systems Support

Let's look at each of these departments in more detail.

Relationship Management: This department is responsible for starting and maintaining Quality Relationships with prospects/customers that match the company's Customer Type. The department has the following sub-groups: Relationship Research, Relationship Development, Communication, and Appreciation/Recognition.
- Relationship Research finds potential prospects who match the company's Customer Type.
- Relationship Development initiates relationships with prospects by offering free value packaged subscriber program.
- The Communication sub-group is entrusted with the task of maintaining on-going dialogue with prospects/customers.
- Appreciation/Recognition helps keep high-quality customers coming back by recognizing them with expressions of appreciation.

Value Creation and Delivery: The people who run this department create and deliver the Value Components of interest to the company's

designated Customer Type. This department has four sub-groups: Value Component Development, Component Assembly, Program Packaging, and Value Delivery.
- The Value Component Development sub-group finds and develops Value Components that will interest the company's prospects and customers.
- The Component Assembly sub-group develops new ways to assemble the company's Value Components, either by employees, and or directly by customers.
- Program Packaging puts together unique configurations of the company's Value Components that will interest all of its customers, or specific individual customers.
- The Value Delivery sub-group guarantees that customers receive the assembled Value Components they ordered.

Ideas and Innovation Development: This department generates, filters, and enhances new ideas and concepts that can be used by the company to create and deliver even greater Unique Value to its customers. The Ideas and Innovation Department has three sub-groups: Idea Generation and Integration, Idea Filtering and Selection, and Innovation Enhancement.
- The Idea Generation and Integration sub-group spends time absorbing information, and combines this data in novel ways to generate new ideas that might be helpful to the company and its customers.
- The Idea Filtering and Selection sub-group reviews the ideas proposed by the first sub-group, and selects those ideas deemed worthy of further development.
- The Innovation Enhancement subgroup takes the selected ideas, conducts extensive research, and further develops the innovations that can be used to create and deliver even greater Unique Value.

Strategy and System Support: The Strategy and System Support Department has four sub-groups: Strategy and System Design, Team Building and Management, Capability Development and Maintenance, and Finance and Administration.
- The Strategy and System Design sub-group makes sure the company is constantly reviewing its primary business models,

strategies and systems. It is also responsible for designing new primary strategies and systems.
- The Team Building and Management sub-group is responsible for creating new teams that plan better strategies and build better systems for each part of the company. This sub-group is also makes sure the teams meet on a regular, consistent basis.
- Capability Development and Maintenance are the builders of the company's systems. They work on teams to ensure the capabilities are developed to support their strategies.
- Finance and Administration handles all of the other activities required to keep the company in business such as financial services and reporting, human resource management, and legal administration.

Of course, this model is simply a guideline. You will have to adapt this model to suit your particular company. However, the model does serve to illustrate the importance of creating an organizational structure centered around your customer, not your products. Most companies fall into strategic and system chaos because they try to develop Quality Relationships with an organizational structure designed to manufacture a Large Number of a Product. In most cases, they either fail miserably, or become extremely frustrated. So don't make the same mistake. Develop an organizational structure focused on creating and delivering Unique Value to a specific Customer Type.

Strategic Planning and System Process Ensures Progress

The Relationship-First Enterprise's structure supports on-going strategic planning and system development. It encourages everyone in the company to take time out from day-to-day money making in order to build a better boat. For every major project in the company (such as new system development, website design, database integration, marketing program creation, and so on), teams are created to plan the strategy, design ideal system models, and determine the required actions. Relationship-First Teams follow this type of process:

Strategic Systems Audit: Before proceeding with any major project, an audit should be conducted to review the company's current situation. This audit will reveal the strengths and weaknesses of the company's existing strategies and systems.

Strategy and System Design Workshops: In these workshops, teams composed of people from different departments in the company meet to develop better strategies and design better systems. Models are created for ideal future strategies and systems. At the end of the workshops, a step-by-step action plan is created, and each team member explains the actions they will take to reach the desired ideal model. They also commit to meeting on a consistent basis to review their progress and develop new strategies and systems.

Progress and Action Session: These are held regularly. The team reviews its progress, reviews and refines the ideal strategy and system models, and decides what actions to take next. By holding these sessions consistently, the team develops a sense of steady progress towards the ideal models it has created.

Putting the Relationship-First Model into Action

To help you understand how the Relationship-First Model can be applied to different kinds of companies, the next chapter, " Relationship-First Enterprise Scenarios," presents five hypothetical organizations that have become Relationship-First Enterprises.

CHAPTER 6:
Relationship-First Enterprise Scenarios

> *"It is possible to fail in many ways... while to succeed is possible only in one way (for which reason also one is easy, and the other difficult—to miss the mark easy, to hit it difficult.)"*
>
> **Aristotle, 384-322 B.C.**

More than 2,300 years ago, Aristotle mused about the fine line between success and failure. It's so easy to miss the mark, and so hard to hit it, Aristotle said. How true! The same reality confronts anyone in business at the start of the 21st century. There are so many ways to fail, and only one way to succeed. In my mind, the only way to succeed in the 21st century is to adopt the Relationship-First Formula, and build a business that delivers Unique Value to a specific Customer Type. To illuminate my belief, and to help you develop your own version of a Relationship-First Enterprise, I present six scenarios based, in part, on real-life companies I've worked with in my consulting practice.

Scenario #1: The Excelsior Drug Company

The Excelsior Drug Company has been using the Product-First Formula since the company was started more than 100 years ago. Excelsior sells a well-known line of over-the-counter drug and healthcare products, including Vymox, the popular headache remedy. In recent years, however, Excelsior has suffered from falling margins, due to increasing competition from generic drug companies, and from downward price pressure exerted by major retail buyers. To turn the tide, Excelsior has decided to adopt the Relationship-First Formula.

As a large company, Excelsior realizes it can ultimately serve dozens of Customer Types, but decided to start with a single one: *Parents With Newborn Babies*. Its goal is to "own" the relationship with this Customer Type by providing them with as much Unique Value as possible. In addition to its traditional infant healthcare products, Excelsior realizes it can provide many new Value Components to *Parents With Newborn Children*. These Value Components include:

- Infant healthcare information (in the form of books, newsletters, videos, audio CDs, and seminars);
- A chatline for new parents (over the Web, and through the telephone);
- Doctor's advice posted on the company's Healthy Baby website;
- Special rates on RESPs, life insurance, and other financial services;
- An extensive online catalogue of products sold by other suppliers, including diapers, baby clothes, baby furniture, toys, and every other possible product needed by new parents;
- Databases listing midwives, nannies, daycare facilities, doctors, and other support services.

To package these Value Components together, Excelsior has created *The Healthy Baby Program*. New parents join the program and receive a free Healthy Baby Kit (filled with products worth more than $100) and free access to Excelsior's Healthy Baby website. In exchange for memberships, parents complete a detailed survey listing all of their concerns and needs as new parents. The information from this survey is entered into Excelsior's central database. The Relationship Management Department at Excelsior uses this information to create customized e-mail messages and individualized web pages that address the unique needs of each member.

Parents With Newborn Babies flock to the Excelsior web site because it contains all of the information they need to keep their baby healthy. At last count, Excelsior had attracted more than two million *Parents*

With Newborn Babies. As well, Excelsior is now making money by selling advertising on its website, and from commissions on the sales of other non-pharmaceutical products sold by third-party suppliers. Excelsior makes this money because it has the best relationship in the marketplace with *Parents With Newborn Babies*. No other company, in no other industry, has such a direct link to this group. As such, if another company wants to reach *Parents With Newborn Babies*, they usually use Excelsior as an intermediary.

The future of Excelsior is now bright because of the Relationship-First Formula. The company has broken out of its product-centric mindset. It no longer sees itself as just a healthcare company. It sees itself as a company that provides Unique Value to *Parents With Newborn Babies*. It now makes money providing thousands of different products and services, not just a handful. As such, it is well equipped to thrive in an age of accelerating change, increasing competition, and instant communication. Change helps Excelsior, because *Parents With Newborn Babies* will always be looking for new things from The Healthy Baby Program. Competition is no longer an issue because Excelsior now makes money from its competitors. And third, instant communication technology such as the Web, e-mail, databases, and high-speed digital printing, allow Excelsior to communicate consistently and inexpensively with *Parents With Newborn Babies* on a mass, customized basis.

Scenario #2: The Pecunia Financial Corporation

The Pecunia Financial Corporation has been struggling to establish itself as a unique financial services company for many years. It sells a host of financial services —tax planning, insurance, mutual funds, online trading, merchant banking, mergers and acquisitions—but it has a hard time standing out as different from thousands of other banks, insurance companies, investment firms, and financial planners.

Until, that is, the president of the company reads this book and realizes the future lay in the Relationship-First Formula. After researching the market, and assessing their core abilities, the team at Pecunia Financial elects to pursue *Business Partners* as their Customer Type.

To attract interest from *Business Partners* around the world, Pecunia develops The Business Partner Success Program. This program is designed to provide *Business Partners* with a never-ending stream of Unique Value to help them deal successfully with the specific problems and challenges they face. The program's Value Components, tailored specifically for business partners, include:

- Business planning seminars and consulting specifically tailored to address the issues faced by business partners;
- Books, audio CDs, videos, and workbooks for business partners;
- Life insurance products that protect one partner if the other partner dies prematurely;
- Succession planning services;
- Tax planning and accounting services;
- Legal services; and
- Access to The Business Partner Success Website.

In most cases, Pecunia does not provide these Value Components directly to *Business Partners*. The Value Creation Department is constantly looking for high-quality companies to provide products and services of value to *Business Partners*. In other words, Pecunia is not limited by the scope of its own products/services and capabilities. By sourcing outside suppliers, Pecunia has unlimited capability to provide Unique Value to its Customer Type.

To initiate relationships with prospects who qualify for The Business Partner Success Program, Pecunia Financial provides *Business Partners* with a free one-on-one Partnership Planning Workshop. During the workshop, the partners identify the personal and business issues they face, and the Pecunia Financial consultant explains the tax and accounting opportunities available to them. By giving away these free workshops, Pecunia has been able to book lots of appointments with Business Partners, and after these extremely helpful workshops, most of the Business Partners sign up for the program. Most of the new clients say: "There are a lot of financial consultants out there, but Pecunia is the only company that deals with the unique problems we face as a business partnership."

To keep in touch with program members and prospects, Pecunia Financial distributes The Business Partner Report, a newsletter in both e-mail and print form. The company has also developed The Business Partner Success Software, and The Business Partner Success Video Series. These products have become so successful, they act as a marketing tool and as a source of revenue. Company president Wilfred Goldsides is also working on a book: The Business Partner Success Formula, to be published next year. Goldsides is quoted widely in the media whenever journalists cover business partnerships.

By building its business around its customers and not around its products and services, Pecunia Financial has also been able to make dramatic improvements in the effectiveness of its computer and information systems. Working together as a team, representatives from all departments in the company developed a model of the ideal information system (IS). To support the Relationship-First Formula, Pecunia's IS system is built around a People Database, not around its manufacturing and accounting activities. Pecunia's People Database contains information about more than 25,000 *Business Partners*. A Value Component database was created, containing all of the 300 Value Components offered by the company. Visitors to The Business Partner Success Website can access the Value Components list and assemble a unique package of products/services that meet their individual needs. As well, information contained in the People Database gives Pecunia Financial the ability to send out customized print and e-mail messages to each of its members. All of the other databases—such as financial reports, trading activity, accounting, and project management—are linked with the central People Database.

By building an IS system based on the Relationship-First Formula, everyone at Pecunia Financial is now much more productive and efficient. With all of its information centered around its customers, Pecunia staff are able to devote more of their time to High-Value Activities (Delivering Value and Creating Value) and significantly less time on Low-Value Activities (Stuff). Pecunia's consultants are now spending more time with customers, and less time on mechanical and repetitive administrative chores.

Most important, Pecunia has been able to differentiate itself from the competition, and establish itself as a unique company with a unique type of customer. It has become easier to get clients, and easier to make money. As well, the people who work for Pecunia are much more focused. They know their job is to create and deliver value to *Business Partners*. They are ready to thrive in the 21st century: a world of accelerating change, increasing competition, and instant communication.

Scenario #3: The Tiger Lilly Tea Co.

Its popular line of teas has made The Tiger Lilly Tea Co. one of the most successful purveyors of tea in the world. However, profits have remained tepid for many years as hundreds of new tea companies have entered the global arena. Tiger Lilly has been searching for a new way to expand its business, and to emerge from the cut-throat low-margin trap of the consumer tea market. As well, Tiger Lilly has been trying to figure out how to take advantage of the technology to sell its products more effectively. However, there are thousands of tea companies on the Internet, and everyone is competing on price. The question is: How can Tiger Lilly stand out in a field boiling over with every imaginable kind of tea?

To answer this question, Tiger Lilly has spend a fortune trying to come up with better kinds of tea, and by analyzing its competitors in the industry. Unfortunately, none of the solutions seem likely to propel Tiger Lilly into higher growth and profitability. But luckily, the executives of Tiger Lilly read this book and realized the Relationship-First Formula can transform the company into a whole new cup of tea.

As the first step in this transformation, Tiger Lilly decides to take its focus off its product—tea—and start its strategic thinking with a type of customer—in this case, *Tea Drinkers*. Tiger Lilly develops a totally new company to provide Unique Value to *Tea Drinkers*. With this single decision, creativity at Tiger Lilly, long stifled by its product-focus mentality, pours forth. Instead of just trying to sell its tea, or make a better kind of tea, Tiger Lilly has decided to provide *Tea Lovers* with hundreds of different Value Components including:

- The world's most extensive database of teas (sold by Tiger Lilly and its competitors);
- A central online store for buying every kind of tea on the market;
- All of the books and videos ever written about tea;
- A review of all the tea-related web sites on the Internet;
- A central catalogue for buying every kind of tea on the market;
- A list of all tea houses around the world; and
- Tours to tea-growing regions of the world.

Tiger Lilly has packaged this program under the name The Tea Lovers Network. The goal is to attract tea lovers to the company by providing non-partisan information about tea. Every person who registers on The Tea Lovers Network receives a free package of exotic teas, and has a chance to win a trip to Japan to participate in a traditional Japanese tea ceremony. During the first year of the program, more than 500,000 tea lovers visit the website and join the network. Members comment: "This is the only place in the world where I can get high-quality information about tea that isn't tied to any particular company. I come to this website because I know everything is here, not just a small part of the tea world."

By attracting *Tea Lovers* to its company, Tiger Lilly has begun to control the flow of information between *Tea Lovers* and tea companies. Tiger Lilly now "owns" the relationship with *Tea Lovers*. With virtually every *Tea Lover* going to its website, Tiger Lilly is able to attract hundreds of its former competitors as customers as well. They pay Tiger Lilly for the right to advertise and sell their teas through the Tea Lovers Network web site, and through The Tea Lovers print catalogue, published twice a year. As well, Tiger Lilly has amassed a massive database of information about *Tea Lovers*. The company knows why people buy certain kinds of tea, what new teas they are looking for, and what brands they like and dislike. Scores of marketers want this information from Tiger Lilly, and are willing to pay large sums of money for the data.

By employing the Relationship-First Formula, Tiger Lilly has made life a lot easier for itself. It doesn't have to worry about low margins on its tea, because most of the time it gives away its tea to get people to join the network. It doesn't have to worry about change, because it knows there will always be *Tea Lovers*. And it doesn't bemoan the spread of instant communications. By making tea consumers more knowledgeable and empowered, instant communications has helped Tiger Lilly attract thousands of new customers, and create dozens of new money-making activities.

Scenario #4: The Golf Course Manager Co.

When George Swing quit his job as national sales manager at The Turf & Green Co., everyone thought he was crazy. After all, Turf & Green was the world's largest supplier of golf course maintenance equipment. But George had a plan. After reading this book, he realized Turf & Green was too firmly wedged into 19th century thinking. The president and top executives could not break out of the Product-First Formula. Whenever George suggested new ways they could expand the Unique Value they offer to customers, the executives looked at him as if he was insane. Even though Turf & Green was facing increasing competition from a field of new competitors, and laboring under falling margins, the executives were totally averse to change. They were hoping the global realities of accelerating change, increasing competition, and instant communication were just passing fads. Looking to get out before the company started to decline, George decided to start his own firm called The Golf Course Manager Co.

The mission of The Golf Course Manager Co. is to help *Golf Course Managers* run a profitable golf course or country club. By joining The Golf Course Profit Program, *Golf Course Managers* are entitled to:
- Participation in The International Golf Course Buyers Group (by bringing *Golf Course Managers* into a group, they are able to demand greater discounts from suppliers);
- Access to discounts of up to 50 percent off all makes and models of golf course maintenance equipment (including equipment from George's former employer Turf & Green)
- State-of-the-art pro shop information management systems;

- Course membership and marketing software;
- Tournament organization and management systems;
- Backshop expertise and facilities;
- Golf course design and construction services;
- Online and traditional marketing and promotional support;
- Golf instruction capabilities;
- Financial services such as insurance and accounting, specially designed for golf course management; and
- Hundreds of other products and services tailored specifically for golf course managers.

To run his business, George only concentrates on two things: developing relationships with *Golf Course Managers*, and sourcing new kinds of Unique Value for them. George travels from course to course meeting with *Golf Course Managers*. (To get the appointments, he offers them a free one-year subscription to Golf Management Monthly). He interviews them and finds out what they need, what their problems are, and what their goals are. With this information, he gets on the telephone and calls his suppliers, or sources new ones. The key point is: George never goes into a sales call with a pre-determined goal. He's not trying to sell his prospects anything. He's just trying to help them in whatever way he can. This attitude helps George keep an open mind, and frees up his creativity. As well, this attitude has made him invaluable to *Golf Course Managers*. They want George around because he is always coming up with new ways to help them.

George does not need a lot of staff, equipment or overhead. He works out of his car most of the time. He has a laptop computer and a cellphone. On his computer, he has a database that keeps track of everything the managers tell him during his meetings. He also has an extensive database of golf course suppliers. As well, George is now working on a website called Course Managers Inter-World. The site will link *Golf Course Managers* with golf course suppliers, and George will act as the go-between because he "owns" the relationship with *Golf Course Managers*.

By starting all of his strategic thinking with a Customer Type, instead of a product, George has greatly expanded his opportunities. It doesn't matter to George that the world is changing faster and faster. The more change the better, George says. It doesn't matter that competition is increasing. Price competition among all of his suppliers just makes George's value-added services more valuable in comparison. And, of course, instant communications technology is the lifeblood of George's business. Using e-mail, web, and cellphone technology, George can stay in close touch with his customers and prospects. In other words, George doesn't fear the global realities of the 21st century. He prospers because of them.

Scenario #5: Icarus Airlines

Icarus Airlines has hit a lot of turbulence in the last few years. With deregulation and increasing competition in the airline industry, Icarus has languished in a commodity trap. Fares for flights have been dropping as consumers use the Web to source the best deals. Capital costs have been increasing as travellers expect more elaborate in-flight services including entertainment systems, larger seating areas, and business facilities. Caught between rising costs and falling prices, the company's margins are falling from the sky.

To propel the airline on a new flight of growth, Icarus Airlines has adopted the Relationship-First Formula. Instead of building its business around its product (airline flights), Icarus has decided to build its business around a specific Customer Type: *High-End Business Travellers*. Icarus will provide hundreds of Unique Value components to the *High-End Business Traveller*. For example, Icarus will help a company president or chief executive officer have a successful business trip from start to finish. Icarus will make all of the travel arrangements: limousines, flight, and rental cars. If needed, Icarus will provide a fully trained attendant to escort the customer for the trip. The Icarus attendant will pack the customer's luggage, make sure all arrangements have been confirmed, carry the baggage, handle all check-ins, drive the rental car, and make sure everything is in order at the destination hotel. Icarus can also provide body guards, security information, and kidnaping insurance if the customer is entering a hostile foreign country. In addition, Icarus has a fleet of private jets that can be rented or leased by its customers.

To initiate relationships with *High-End Business Travellers*, Icarus offers all CEOs and presidents a free flight to anywhere in North America on one of its private jets. The prospects are escorted by an Icarus attendant who explains the details of The Business Traveller Executive Program. If they join the program, they receive a score of benefits including:
- An Icarus Diamond Credit Card (with an automatic $1 million line-of-credit);
- A subscription to the Icarus Business Traveller Bulletin (which provides customized information unique to the specific travel and business needs of the reader);
- A free satellite telephone, and one-year of free call time;
- Membership at Icarus Spa & Lounge facilities at more than 100 airports;
- Exclusive access to premium insurance products designed for high-end executives who travel extensively; and
- Affiliate memberships at more than 500 private clubs around the world.

By creating The Business Traveller Executive Program, Icarus has taken itself out of the competitive commodity trap. Its customers have no interest in comparing prices with other suppliers, because there isn't anyone who provides the kind of program offered by Icarus. Icarus can charge whatever the market will bear, and in most cases, the customer never bothers to scrutinize the bill. They're just happy that someone has come along to handle all of their travel needs, not just one part of it. They are able to go on a business trip with a minimum of paperwork, hassle, and worry. They arrive at their business meetings rested and relaxed, and ultimately, they make more sales and more money.

By providing Unique Value to *High-End Business Travellers*, Icarus has secured the primary relationship in the marketplace with presidents and CEOs. As a result, Icarus makes a fortune selling advertising for its magazines, web sites, and inflight entertainment systems. Icarus also makes a commission booking flights on other airlines for its members. As well, it receives commissions from hotels, car rental agencies, security companies, insurance firms, and most of its other suppliers. Icarus is making so much money from its customers, its traditional business (airline flights) has become just an excuse to offer these other products and services. In fact, Icarus is thinking of getting another company to manage its airline while it concentrates on delivering Unique Value to *High-End Business Travellers*.

Scenario #6: VIXVAC Heating & Air-Conditioning

VIXVAC Heating & Air Conditioning is a very successful manufacturer of commercial heating and air-conditioning equipment. VIXVAC has five manufacturing plants, 3,000 employees, and thousands of customers around the world. Although business has been good in recent years, the president of VIXVAC, Bart Faringfield, wants to grow the business further. He has thought about developing new heating and air-conditioning units, or about expanding into Asian markets, but he's not too sure. Margins on his existing products are slim, and the cost to develop new technology is high. As well, competition in foreign markets is growing as new manufacturers enter the picture. Fortunately, Faringfield had the good sense to read this book, and realized he should abandon his obsolete product focus and develop a company that could thrive in the 21st century.

Faringfield started by analyzing his existing market. He realized quickly that the company's most important customers are *Consulting Engineers* who work on commercial construction projects. These engineers are the people who choose the heating and air-conditioning units for projects. In most cases, they are looking for the lowest price because they think all HVAC (heating, ventilation, & air-conditioning) equipment is the same. They don't care what company they buy HVAC equipment from, as long as they get the lowest price.

Faringfield realized he has to develop a higher quality relationship with *Consulting Engineers* in order to grow his business. He realized VIXVAC has to increase the amount of Unique Value it delivers to these people if it ever hopes to break out of its commodity trap. To this end, Faringfield created The HVAC Selector Program designed to help *Consulting Engineers* do their job easier and better. The program comprises the following Value Components:

- The HVAC Selector Software which enables *Consulting Engineers* to spec out an HVAC project in a matter of minutes, instead of hours;
- The HVAC Selector Series of seminars, videos, DVDs, websites, books, and reports;
- The HVAC Selector Report, which provides up-to-date information on the HVAC industry as it relates to Consulting Engineers;
- Direct access to hundreds of HVAC-related products and services through the HVAC Selector Online Network, a website sponsored by VIXVAC.

To promote the program, Faringfield ran advertising and wrote articles to appear in trade publications and websites popular with *Consulting Engineers*. Direct mail packages were distributed to more than 20,000 of these engineers worldwide. As well, VIXVAC also sponsored the International Consulting Engineers Conference in Des Moine, Iowa. To attract *Consulting Engineers*, VIXVAC offered them a free copy of The HVAC Selector Software, and free access to a database of more than 5,000 technical HVAC papers. When a prospect signs up for the program, VIXVAC dispatches a consultant to meet with the *Consulting Engineer*. During the first meeting, the VIXVAC consultant helps the *Consulting Engineer* spec out an HVAC project using the free software. He or she also shows the *Consulting Engineer* how to get the most value out of the VIXVAC website.

With regards to its HVAC products, VIXVAC has also made significant breakthroughs. Instead of marketing specific models and units, VIXVAC has divided all of its products into their component parts. *Consulting Engineers* can now come on to the VIXVAC website and assemble HVAC equipment that meets their custom specifications. These unique units can then be quickly assembled by VIXVAC and shipped within days. As such, VIXVAC is once again able to deliver Unique Value to its customers.

Adopting the Relationship-First Formula has also helped VIXVAC bring unity to its information systems (IS). While it was using the Product-First Formula, VIXVAC did not have a clear vision for its IS capabilities. The engineering and manufacturing departments used their own software. Accounting had its own system, and so did the marketing department. In fact, the company had more than 30 different software platforms. No wonder everyone at VIXVAC was frustrated. They spent too much time transferring information from one system to another. As a result, information went missing, or became inaccurate. Customer service suffered.

Using the Relationship-First Formula, however, it became very clear how to develop the IS system. The system was developed around its customers, not around its products. All databases were created using the same platform so the information could shared across the company, in all departments. The new IS system allows VIXVAC staff to spend more time delivering value and creating value. It also gives them much more information about their customers, and enables them to respond quickly when a customer has a question. Moreover, the IS system also gives *Consulting Engineers* the ability to work with VIXVAC over the Web on an HVAC project from start to finish.

Using the Relationship-First Formula has increased the number of units VIXVAC sells to *Consulting Engineers*. Previously, VIXVAC only got orders for about 15 percent of the proposals it wrote. Now VICVAX scores about 40 percent. *Consulting Engineers* choose VIXVAC more often because they see a distinct difference between the company and other HVAC suppliers. As well, they like working with VIXVAC because its employees are so helpful and easy to interact with over the Web and in person.

Indeed, VIXVAC has a warm and cool future ahead in the 21st century. No matter how much technology changes, VIXVAC will continue to build on its relationship with *Consulting Engineers*. No matter how much competition enters the market, VIXVAC can always differentiate itself by adding more components to its stable of Unique Value. And no matter what kind of instant communication technology emerges in the future, VIXVAC will be able to use it to communicate more effectively with *Consulting Engineers*.

Making the Transformation

As the scenarios presented in this chapter illustrate, transforming your company into a Relationship-First Enterprise first requires a change of perspective: from a focus on your products/services to a focus on a particular kind of customer. In most cases, the Customer Type you choose will be one you are already serving. As such, you will not have to build an entirely new company. You will just start your strategic thinking with your Customer Type and work your way backwards to specific products and services (which we call Value Components). In this way, you can better assess the value your existing products and services provide to customers, and more easily see what improvements you need to make to existing products, and what new products you need to introduce. All you have to do is turn your head around 180 degrees.

Of course, building a Relationship-First Enterprise requires more than just a change in perspective. In the next chapter, "Your Strategic Transformation," I explain step by step how to change your company from a 19th century anachronism to a Relationship-First Enterprise ready to thrive in the 21st century.

CHAPTER 7:
The Transformation

"Furthermore, we have not even to risk the adventure alone, for the heroes of all time have gone before us. The labyrinth is thoroughly known. We have only to follow the thread of the hero path, and where we had thought to find abomination, we shall find god...And where we had thought to be alone, we will be with all the world."

Joseph Campbell, *The Power of Myth*

To transform your business into a Relationship-First Enterprise, you embark on a hero's adventure. You forsake the security of the past, and strike out in a new direction. But fear not. As Joseph Campbell says, the labyrinth is thoroughly known. Many people before you, when faced with global change, have transformed their business. People in the early 1800s had to adapt to the new dictates of the Industrial Revolution. They had to change the way they did business. They had to change their paradigms. And after a lot of trial and error, no doubt, they succeeded. So, as you enter the labyrinth of change, just follow the thread of their path, and you too will find your company's true calling in the 21st century.

The transformation into a Relationship-First Enterprise is, in fact, a straightforward step-by-step process. You assemble a strategic team of people from inside and outside your company. You choose a type of customer. You figure out what unique value components to provide them. You develop a promotional idea to communicate clearly the benefits you provide. You decide what free value to give away to attract prospects who match your Customer Type profile. You craft a unified message to communicate. You establish a consistent graphic identity. You build a database to store information about your customers and prospects. You build an information system centered around your people database. You develop systems to quickly assemble your value components. You promote your company through digital and traditional media. And you foster long-term, quality relationships with your customers.

That's all there is to it. You don't need an MBA from Harvard to transform your company. In fact, most MBAs should put aside their academic mumbo jumbo and take these basic steps. They would save everyone a lot of time and money. So don't be put off by the simplicity of this process. I've spent 25 years working through all of the complexity to make it simple on your behalf. I've developed strategies and systems with more than 4,000 companies, and this experience has taught me what works and what doesn't. So don't skip a step. Follow them as they are presented.

Step #1: Create Your Relationship-First Team

To develop effective strategies and build unified systems, create a Relationship-First Team. The team will work together to choose your Customer Type, identify your Value Components, and develop your Controlling Promotional Idea. The team will also design model systems (such as database or website systems) and work on their development.

Members of your Relationship-First Team can come from inside and outside of your company. Ideally, every major department of your company should be represented. If you have valued consultants and suppliers, put them on your team. (Remember: The Relationship-First Enterprise does not try to do everything itself. It's always looking for help from the world at large). As a rule, the team should comprise about eight to 12 people.

To maintain the integrity and enthusiasm of the team, ensure the following conditions are met:

- Each member participates in the development of strategies and systems;
- Each member takes responsibility for the actions required to implement the new strategies and build the new systems;
- Progress and Action Sessions are planned and booked at the conclusion of each meeting;
- These sessions are held at the time and date they were scheduled. (They are not delayed, postponed or cancelled arbitrarily.)
- Progress is acknowledged and celebrated at each Progress and Action Session.
- Each team member takes responsibility for further actions at each session.

The Four Strategic Principles: To keep your Relationship-First Team together over the long term, everyone must subscribe to these four basic principles:

1. We must build our business around our customers, not around our products and services. We must start all strategic thinking with a specific Customer Type.
2. We must give away value to start new relationships.
3. We must take time out regularly to plan better strategies and build better systems.
4. We will only implement new strategies and systems if they help us foster Quality Relationships with our customers, and increase our ability to create and deliver Unique Value.

Your company will quickly become a Relationship-First Enterprise if everyone on your team buys into these principles. If they don't, your business will not move forward in any significant way.

Create Your Relationship-First Enterprise Team:
Three Key Points
- Your Relationship-First Team can have representatives from inside and outside of your company. Every major department should be represented.
- Plan new strategies and build new systems as a team. To maintain

momentum and increase motivation, your Relationship-First Team should meet on a regular, consistent basis.
- To make progress as a team, every member must subscribe to the Four Strategic Principles.

Step #2: Choose Your Customer Type

The first and most important task for a Relationship-First Team is to choose a Customer Type. This decision will determine the direction of your company for years to come. So choose carefully. Don't rush your decision. Look at all the possible customer types before you make up your mind.

To choose your Customer Type, list all of the different markets you currently serve, or new markets you would like to serve. You might identify only a few Customer Types, or you may list 20 or more. When you have completed your list, prioritize each type. Ask yourself: "If we could only have one Customer Type, which one would we choose? If we had to give up a Customer Type, which would we discard?" Work your way through the list until you have prioritized the segments from best to worst. For example, let's say you own a printing company. Your list of eight Customer Types might look like this:

1. Associations
2. Design agencies
3. Small business
4. Banks
5. Government departments
6. Insurance companies
7. Advertising agencies
8. Manufacturers

From this exercise, you may decide to choose *Associations* as your Customer Type. You realize your printing company is ideally suited to create and deliver Unique Value to *Associations*. You have the capabilities to handle newsletters, membership materials, websites, membership mailings, and other products and services required by *Associations*.

Choosing *Associations* is a good start, but you need to take the process further. To reflect the spirit of the Relationship-First Formula, your Customer Type must be a type of person, not a type of company or organization. After all, you have a relationship with a type of person, not a type of organization. As such, simply expand the definition of your Customer Type. Instead of *Associations*, your Customer Type is actually *Association Managers*. They are the people who will buy your services, and write the checks. The key point is: Your Customer Type should be a type of person, not a type of company or organization.

When you have chosen your first Customer Type, you may be inclined to look longingly at the other types on your list. You might ask: "But what about *Design Agencies*, *Small Business*, and *Banks*? Are we going to abandon customers we have made money from for years? Are we only going to focus on *Association Managers*?" To answer these questions, you have to assess the size of the market, and your core capabilities. Can you build an entire business around *Association Managers*? Is the market big enough, or lucrative enough? If so, you might decide to focus strictly on *Association Managers*. If the market is too small, you might decide to purse two Customer Types: *Association Managers*, and *Print Production Managers at Design Firms*. However, if you choose two or more Customer Types, you must treat them as two totally separate businesses. This means you will develop Unique Value components for each of these Customer Types, and create completely separate Controlling Promotional Ideas.

If you have a small business, you are best advised to pursue a single Customer Type; your resources are not sufficient to handle more than one market. If you work for a larger company, such as a Fortune 500 corporation, you may pursue dozens, if not hundreds of Customer Types. You have the resources small businesses don't have. Regardless, I do suggest you begin this process by choosing just one Customer Type, no matter how big your company is, or how enticing secondary markets may appear. Choose one Customer Type, and work your way through your transformation. Once you have developed your Relationship-First skills, you can apply them to as many different Customer Types as you want.

When you have chosen your Customer Type, assess the market conditions. Does another company already own the relationship with your chosen Customer Type? If so, you either chose another one, or become even more specialized. For example, you might choose *Computer Users* as your Customer Type. After researching the market, you may realize a lot of companies are targeting *Computer Users*. You may need to become even more specialized. Instead of trying to develop a relationship with all the computer users in the world, you may focus on *Users of Apple Computers*. You will provide them with specialized knowledge, and specific products and services that meet the unique needs of Apple computer users. In this way, you zero in on a very specific market. In fact, the more specialized your Customer Type, the more focused and successful your company will probably become.

Once you have chosen your Customer Type, you are well on your way to becoming a Relationship-First Enterprise. By starting your strategic thinking with a Customer Type, and not with your products and services, you will immediately notice a difference in your company. You will start talking about how to increase the Unique Value you deliver to these kinds of customers. You will start identifying potential customers more easily. And you'll have a much clearer idea of where your company is headed in the future.

Choose Your Customer Type: Three Key Points
- Choosing your Customer Type is your most important strategic decision.
- Your Customer Type should be a type of person, not a type of company (For example: *Association Managers*, not *Associations*).
- The more specialized your Customer Type, the greater your chance for success (For example, *Users of Apple Computers*, not *Computer Users*).

Step #3: List Your Value Components

As a Relationship-First Enterprise, your company will thrive in the 21st century if you provide your Customer Type with a never-ending stream of Unique Value. You will deliver this Unique Value by offering your customers an increasing number of Value Components. Your customers will assemble these Value Components into unique packages that suit their individual needs and interests. Your next step, then, is to create a list of the Value Components you could provide your Customer Type.

As an example, let's pretend you are a documentary film and television producer. In the past, you had a product focus. You produced documentaries about the major events of the 20th century. You want to become a Relationship-First Enterprise, so you choose *20th Century History Buffs* as your Customer Type. You develop a list of Value Components that appeal to *20th Century History Buffs* including:

- electronic news stories (TV and radio)
- historical films
- interviews (TV and radio)
- newspaper and magazine articles
- photographs
- history books
- 20th century historians and experts
- research and analytical papers
- historical sites
- museums and their 20th century contents

As you can see, all of these Value Components are interesting to *20th Century History Buffs*. And it's just a partial list. You can just keep adding components as you think of them or discover them. You'll never run out of ideas. As well, you'll never run out of ways to put these components together. You can assemble them as:
- A multimedia database about the 20th century available on the Web and DVD.
- Documentaries, films and television shows about the 20th century;
- Customized encyclopedias and text books about the 20th century;
- A historical travel advisory service (delivered in dozens of different ways);
- A bureau of speakers who talk about the 20th century.

As you can see, by choosing a Customer Type, and listing Unique Value in terms of components, you (the documentary producer) now have the ability to create even more products and services. And that's another irony of this process. By starting with a Customer Type, you actually end up with the ability to create even more products.

So start now, and write down all of the different components of Unique Value you could provide your Customer Type. Start with your existing products and services, and then add more. Don't hesitate to add something you don't currently have the ability to deliver. Other companies or organizations may be able to produce it for you.

Just let your creativity flow. As a Relationship-First Enterprise, you aren't encumbered by the narrow vision of your existing products and services. All you have to ask yourself is, "What would excite, entertain, interest, help, improve, empower, and satisfy my Customer Type?" As well, remember this is just the beginning. As you get to know your Customer Type better, you'll discover a myriad of other Value Components to serve them. It's likely you'll never run out of ideas.

When you have made your list, check off the items you already create and deliver to your customers. Then choose other components you would like to offer next. Keep this in mind: You don't have to start creating hundreds of new Value Components. You might just start with the Value Components you deliver now. Or you might just offer a single component at first. It doesn't matter. At this point, it's only important that you view all of your products and services as components.

For example, our documentary filmmaker could look at his existing library of films, and divide the content into smaller components of different scenes, events, and stories. Instead of looking at each film as a separate entity (product) unto itself, he sees each movie as simply one particular way of assembling different components. This perspective (seeing your products and services comprised of smaller constituent components) will help you develop more flexible information, marketing, and assembly systems in your company.

At the completion of this step, you should have a comprehensive list of Value Components you could offer to your Customer Type. You should have selected the Value Components you want to initially create and deliver to your customers. As well, you should be working on dividing your existing products and services into their constituent component parts.

List Your Value Components: Three Key Points
- Create a list of all the products and services (Value Components) that might appeal to your Customer Type.
- Don't limit yourself to Value Components you can produce. Suppliers and strategic partners could supply additional Value Components.
- Divide your products and services into their constituent components. This will allow you to better serve the unique needs of individual customers.

Step #4: Develop Your Controlling Promotional Idea

To attract prospects who match your Customer Type, you must communicate a clearly defined, and unified promotion. This promotion, which I call a Controlling Promotional Idea, will help you stand out from the competition, and bring order to all of your marketing activities. For example, let's say you have chosen *Dentists* as your Customer Type. To attract dentists to your company, you develop a Controlling Promotional Idea called The Dentist Support Network. The Dentist Support Network is a program that helps dentists succeed in their practice. If they join the network, they gain access to hundreds of different Value Components including:
- Online discussion forums with other dentists;
- Access to thousands of dentistry research papers;
- Discounts on dentist equipment, computer hardware and software, insurance, travel, and conferences.
- An online advisory committee ready to answer dentist management questions; and
- Dozens of other products and services useful to dentists.

To encourage prospective *Dentists* to learn more about The Dentist Support Network, they are offered a free subscription to The Dentist Support Magazine, and the chance to win a $100,000 video dentistry system. To get the free magazine, they simply visit The Dentist Support Network website and fill out the membership application form. When they come to the site, they quickly see all the amazing benefits of the network, and keep coming back again and again.

Creating a Controlling Promotional Idea such as The Dentist Support Network is important for a number of reasons. First, the concept lends a sense of unity to your marketing programs. All of your marketing tools—advertising, brochures, news releases, direct mail, sales letters, newsletters, websites, and e-mail—communicate the same message and benefits. Two, the concept makes it easier for your prospects and customers to understand what you offer, and how it will benefit them. Instead of seeing a confusing mass of different messages, products, and services, they will see a neatly packaged program. Three, a Controlling Promotional Idea protects you from accelerating change. No matter what technology arises, or new consumer tastes emerge, you can always package your Unique Value under the same program. You can use the concept for 10, 20, 30 years or more.

To develop your Controlling Promotional Idea, do the following:
- Come up with a name that identifies either the Customer Type and/or the major benefit of the program;
- Determine the three major benefits the program will provide to your Customer Type;
- Apply the controlling promotional concept to all of your marketing tools;
- Plan to use the controlling promotional concept for many years, no matter what changes you make to the Unique Value you provide;
- If you have more than one Customer Type, create a different Controlling Promotional Idea for each one.

Develop Your Controlling Promotional Idea: Three Key Points
- A Controlling Promotional Idea helps you stand out from the competition, and brings order to all of your marketing activities.

- A Controlling Promotional Idea helps you clearly communicate the benefits you provide to your Customer Type.
- A Controlling Promotional Idea is future-proof because you can use it for many years no matter what changes occur in technology, in the marketplace, or in your company.

Step #5: Determine The Free Value To Give Away

Instead of trying to get through the impervious wall set up by prospects, the Relationship-First Enterprise gives away value to attract new prospects. The Relationship-First Enterprise realizes it must give prospects something free to start new relationships with them. This free value can take many forms—free seminars, books, advice, memberships, cellphones, trips, computers, or just plain cash. The key point is: You have to give this value away for free <u>before</u> you make your sales pitch. Otherwise, the prospect will run for the hills.

In my business, we offer our prospects a free Big Idea Starter Session. Instead of making a sales pitch, we meet with prospects to help them develop and package a BIG Idea. Even if they never talk to us again, the prospects get something they can use; in this case, a new business or promotional idea.

Of course, we are very careful to qualify our prospects before we give them the free value. We ask them a lot of questions first to make sure they match our Customer Type profile. We determine if they are committed to improving their strategies and systems. In other words, we don't throw out this free value to every person who comes along. And we do expect something in return. They have to spend 90 minutes with us. The main point is: When we find a qualified prospect, the free value gets us in the door. This gives us the opportunity to start a relationship with them.

So figure out what type of free value would attract prospects who match your Customer Type. You can give away something of very little value, or something quite expensive—either in time or money. But don't play the cheapskate. You might not get the result you want. As well, don't delude yourself. Don't offer a free sales pitch or a free brochure. They aren't valuable to your prospects. They are only valuable to you. Start thinking from the perspective of your Customer Type. Think about what they want. Not what you want.

Determine The Free Value To Give Away: Three Key Points
- To attract prospects, you must first give away free value.
- The free value can take many forms, such as free seminars, books, advice, memberships, cellular telephones, trips, computers, or even cash.
- The greater the value you give away for free, the more prospects you will attract.

Step #6: Craft A Unified Message

Once you have created your Controlling Promotional Idea and determined the free value you will give away, you will develop tools—such as presentations, brochures, websites, e-mail, advertising, publicity, and direct mail—to communicate with them. However, as a Relationship-First Enterprise, it's important that your company communicate a unified message. All of your communications tools must tell the same story. You must use the same words, the same vocabulary, and the same images.

Why is it important to communicate a unified message? A consistent message tells the world you are an organized, professional, and focused company. It also helps your customers and prospects quickly appreciate the Unique Value you provide—the first major hurdle in the sales and marketing process.

To achieve a high standard of consistent communication, your core message must emanate from a single source. I call this core document *The Definitive Article*. To develop The Definitive Article, have a writer interview you and members of your team. Have the writer produce the first draft of the article, and present it to you and the team. Work together to resolve any discrepancies or divergent viewpoints you have about your story. Decide exactly which words and phrases best represent the style and unique nature of your company. Through the process of writing, editing, and revisions, you will arrive at the final draft: The Definitive Article.

When it's completed, The Definitive Article is the manifesto of your company's marketing programs. When developing content for a brochure or a website, simply refer back to the article. This speeds up the process, and helps you avoid wasting time and money. As well, if you make a change to your business, you simply edit The Definitive Article accordingly, and then make the changes to your existing marketing materials.

Craft A Unified Message: Three Key Points
- To project a professional image, a Relationship-First Enterprise tells a consistent, unified message in all of its communications.
- To develop a unified message, you need to write a document called The Definitive Article before you develop other marketing tools such as brochures and websites.
- When completed, The Definitive Article becomes the manifesto of your company's marketing programs. All communications reflect the content of The Definitive Article.

Step #7: Establish Your Graphic Identity

The Relationship-First Enterprise projects a consistent graphic identity to its Customer Type. All of its communications tools—such as business cards, letterhead, brochures, advertising, and websites—look like they belong to the same family. They use the same images, colors, typefaces, and layout.

To achieve this kind of consistent graphic identity, start a Style Control Guide. This a binder that contains a sample of every communications tool you use, including fax cover forms, database screen printouts, presentation templates, and any other items that are visible to customers, suppliers and employees. By putting these documents together in one place, you will see if they are consistent or mismatched. You can then work towards a consistent style for all of your communications tools.

To assemble your Style Control Guide, put someone on your team in charge of it. Make them the Style Control Guide administrator. This person will work with graphic designers to establish the Style Control Guide rules, and bring all of your communications tools in line with the standard. Once you have this standard, you will make it known to everyone in the company. You can also create standard templates that allow people to quickly create new communications tools that meet the standards in the Style Control Guide.

Like The Definitive Article, the Style Control Guide is a single source from which everything else emanates. It gives the Relationship-First Enterprise greater flexibility while still retaining consistency.

Establish Your Identity: Three Key Points
- All of your communications tools, such as business cards, letterhead, brochures, advertising, and websites, must use the same images, colors, typefaces, and layout.
- To achieve a consistent graphic identity, create a binder that contains a sample of all of your communications tools. This is called a Style Control Guide binder.
- Establish Style Control Guide rules for the standard images, colors, typefaces, and layout of all your communications tools.

Step #8: Build Your People Database

In the Relationship-First Enterprise, all information and computer systems are designed around customers, not products or services. As such, the first capability you need to create is your People Database. This is a database containing the names of all of your customers and prospects. You will build all of your other databases and communications tools around this database.

To get started, you need to select a database software program. At this point, it does not really matter which program you select, but I do recommend you use generic database software, not some kind of pre-configured contact manager or sales automation tool. The generic database software will give you more flexibility, and allow you to transfer the information more easily to another platform later if required.

If you already have one or more customer databases, you will have to bring them together into one centralized database. (This is a key principle: You must have one People Database, not several spread out across the organization.) As well, you may need to enter business card information into the database, clean up duplications, correct errors, and fill in missing data. This is a big job initially, but once it is completed you will have an accurate, up-to-date, and centralized People Database. You will also be ready to build an integrated information system, with your customers and prospect as the central focus.

Start Your People Database: Three Key Points
- In the Relationship-First Enterprise, all information and computer systems are designed around customers, not products or services.
- The centre of your information system must be your People Database.
- You must have one People Database, not several spread out across the organization.

Step #9: Integrate Your Information Systems

For your company to become a Relationship-First Enterprise, everyone in the organization must be able to share and communicate information easily and quickly. You need an information system that lets you spend most of your time creating and delivering unique value, and decrease the time you spend on low-value activities. You need a system that enhances your creativity and helps you foster quality relationships with your customers. You also need a system that allows you and your customers to quickly assemble your value components. This system acts as the brain and central nervous system of your organization.

I've learned you can develop this capability only if you have an integrated information system. By "integrated," I mean a system that runs on a single platform and makes all of the company's information available in one centralized location. To my surprise, I've discovered that very few companies have an integrated system. When I conduct a strategic system audit, I usually find that companies have a fragmented system. Information is scattered across the organization in different databases, often running on different platforms and all the employees are frustrated because they can't get the information from one platform to another. Because their systems are fragmented, these companies waste a lot of time and money, and miss a lot of opportunities.

That's why I recommend that you and your team plan and build and integrated information system. To do this, observe these principles:

1. *Make your customers the central focus.*
Once again, let me emphasize that the central database of your system should be the list of all the people involved in your company: customers, suppliers, employees, strategic partners, and everyone else. We call this your people database.

2. *Put your vision ahead of your technology.*
Your vision should drive the decisions about the type of technology you acquire instead of your technology dictating the limits of your vision. Start with an ideal system model, then choose technology that allows you to achieve this model.

3. *Work together as a team.*
Your team should work together to provide direction to your IT consultants and in-house professionals. Do not leave your computer consultants stranded. Give them direction.

4. *Use only one software platform.*
Once you have chosen your database platform, all of the information used by the company (to the maximum extent possible) should be stored and used on that platform.

5. *Avoid proprietary systems.*
Although many proprietary systems (such as sales-contact-management software) are well designed and loaded with thousands of functions, they do not necessarily serve the strategic long-term needs of the

organization. They often require you to exchange long-term growth for short-term gains in productivity.

6. *Store each type of information in its own database file.*
Each type of information (such as your list of products or your list of correspondence) should be stored in its own database. For examples, you should not have a separate database for people who live in New York and another for people who live in Los Angeles. They should all be stored in your centralized people database.

7. *Use databases to manage all major activities of the company.*
To achieve the highest levels of flexibility and productivity, use databases to organize all of your company's activities, including scheduling, filing, billing, promotion, inventory management, and teamwork.

8. *Be an author, not a user.*
With advances in technology, most database systems have become much easier for the layperson to build and manage. It's no longer necessary to have a computer expert create new databases, new reports, or new database relationships. As a result, it's important for the people in your company to develop the confidence to take on these tasks themselves.

It's amazing how many companies build information systems without a plan. This is like building a house without first having an architect create a blueprint. And that's why their systems are so fragmented. They didn't start with an ideal system model. They started building without a clear path of where they were headed. Don't make the same mistake. Before you build an information system, work together as a team to create an ideal system model.

Integrate Your Information Systems:
Three Key Points
1. To create a Relationship-First Enterprise, you must have an integrated information system built around your people database.
2. An integrated system will increase the amount of time you can spend creating and delivering unique value and decrease the time you spend on low-value activities.

3. Create your ideal system model before you choose software and start building your system.

Step #10:
Develop Interactive Communications Tools

To build a Relationship-First Enterprise, you must be able to communicate easily with your customers. You must be able to create and deliver information of value to your customers using the telephone, e-mail, fax, or the Web, or through traditional means such as print/mail and personal one-to-one contact.

The key point is: You must communicate with your customers using the medium of their choice, not just in the manner you find most convenient or economical. If your customers want to deal with you over the Web, you need to develop interactive Web sites. If they want to deal with you in person, you have to meet with them face to face. It's likely you'll have to develop the capability to communicate efficiently in most media if you want to serve the unique needs of all your customers. You'll have to offer your customers a choice.

If you want to communicate interactively using a multitude of media, it's vitally important that you develop an integrated information system first. Such a system will give you the ability to sort and output information quickly by e-mail, over the Web, or on a color laser printer. It's best to visualize your information/database system as the brain of your organization. Communications tools such as the Web and e-mail are the mouth/voice. If the brain is powerful and well organized, high-quality content will come out of the mouth. If the system is fragmented and disorganized, only gibberish will come out of the company's mouth.

In addition, it's important that your information and communication systems give you the ability to communicate on a mass but customized basis. In other words, you need to be able to quickly send out a lot of information that is unique to each customer or prospect. You should be able to (with a minimum of effort):

- Send out individual letters, faxes, and emails;
- Send out individualized mass mailings in print and email formats;
- Support personal Web pages for each individual customer;
- Create customized product brochures and sales sheets in print, email, or on the Web;
- Provide customers with electronic forms for all of the administrative functions involved in your company; and
- Gather research data from your customers and prospects in a variety of ways.

In my book *Strategic Marketing for the Digital Age,* I explain in detail all of the digital and traditional communications tools available to a Relationship-First Enterprise. These tools include telephone-based interactive voice response (IVR), email, the Web, private online networks, interactive kiosks, wireless devices, pagers, and push channels. As we move into the twenty-first century, many new communication tools will be introduced, such as smart phones, wireless devices, and social media. As a Relationship-First Enterprise, your company will develop these new capabilities as your customers demand them.

Develop Interactive Communications Tools:
Three Key Points
1. To build a Relationship-First Enterprise, you must be able to communicate easily with your customers.
2. You must be able to create and deliver information of value to your customers using the telephone, email, faxes, or the Web, or through traditional means such as print/mail and personal one-to-one contact.
3. You must communicate with your customers using the medium of their choice, not just in the manner you find most convenient or economical.

Step #11: Launch Your Controlling Promotional Idea

When you have completed the first ten steps, you are ready to promote your company. You need to communicate to your customer the free value you provide, as well as some initial information about your unique value. This is done by employing the many proactive marketing tools and methods available to you, such as

- Advertising on billboards, radio, television, magazines, and Web sites;
- Newsletters and direct mail;
- Media publicity;
- Sponsorship of events;
- Email and fax broadcasts;
- Networking and strategic partnerships; and
- Through dozens of other proactive media and channels.

As I said, your goal is to make your customer type aware of your controlling promotional idea and the free value you offer. Because you have selected a distinct customer type, it's much easier to choose the right channels to promote your company. For example, let's say you've chosen worm pickers as your customer type. Your company, the Worm Picker People, provides worm pickers with the Global Worm Picker Program. To get them to join the program, you offer them a free electronic worm finder and a chance to win a trip for two to the World Worm Picker Expo in Dunghill, Australia.

To promote your program, you place ads in *Worm Picker World* magazine, you write articles for the *Worm Picker Journal*, and you sponsor a worm picker forum on Facebook. You also send out a direct-mail piece using a mailing list purchased from the Worm Picker Federation. This campaign reaches just about every worm picker in the world. When they hear about your program and the free offer, thousands of worm pickers make their way to your web site WormNet.com. They fill out a form to apply for the program, and information about them is entered instantly into your database. Now you have detailed information about thousands of worm pickers. You can now create customized emails and print packages all about your unique value components—worm-picker equipment, clothes, headlights, videos, books, worm market data, and much more. Within a few months, your campaign is a huge success. You now own the relationship with worm pickers. You have wormed your way into their hearts. What's more, you've even become an honorary member of the Worm Picker Foundation.

Like the Worm Picker People, you must take these steps to launch your controlling promotional idea:
- Find the media – newspapers, magazines, radio and television shows – used by your customer type.
- Determine the community events and associations frequented by your customer type.
- Find strategic partners who also market to your customer type, or could lead you to them.
- Get mailing lists of people who match your customer type, or could lead you to them.
- Find all websites, social media groups, and other online venues frequented by your customer type.
- Create promotional copy, advertising, and media information about your controlling promotional idea.
- Run your promotional campaign in the appropriate media.

Depending on your customer type, you may need to use only one or two of these methods to reach your prospects. You may meet them by making one speech or by getting introductions from your associates. You may know many of them already from your existing business. In any case, by having a clear customer type, you will be able to focus your marketing resources, and it will be much easier to attract quality prospects to your company.

Launch Your Controlling Promotional Idea:
Three Key Points
1. Your goal is to communicate to your customer type the free value you provide so you can initiate a relationship with them.
2. To communicate with your customer type, you must employ proactive marketing tools and methods.
3. Because you have selected a distinct customer type, it's much easier to choose the right channels to promote your company.

Step #12: Foster Long-Term, Quality Relationships

The mission of a Relationship-First Enterprise is to develop quality relationships by providing a never-ending stream of unique value to a specific type of customer. Once you have attracted a high-quality customer, the relationship must grow and endure. To foster a long-term, quality relationship, you must
- Show your customers you appreciate their patronage;
- Communicate on a regular, consistent basis;
- Treat each customer as an individual;
- Constantly add new value that will interest your customers;
- Reward long-term customers with special programs;
- Respect their privacy (don't sell off information you have about them without their permission):
- Listen to them, ask for feedback, and act on the feedback;
- Always provide value before expecting something in return; and
- Remember that the customer is in control of the relationship, not you.

Fostering long-term, quality relationships is an art and a skill. It also requires the right capabilities. That's why I put so much emphasis on your people database. This database is the collective memory of your organization. It contains everything you know about your customers. The more you know and record in the database, the more you can do for them, and the more unique value you can create and deliver. That's why you also need to communicate with customers using a variety of media. The easier it is for you to communicate, the better the relationship you'll have with your customers.

Foster Long-Term Quality Relationships:
Three Key Points
1. To foster a long-term, quality relationship, you must show appreciation for a customer's patronage and communicate on a regular, consistent basis.
2. Your people database is the collective memory of your organization. It contains everything you know about your customer.
3. The more you know and record in the database about your

customers, the more unique value you can create and deliver to them.

The Hero's Journey, Continued

When you have completed these twelve steps, your company will be a Relationship-First Enterprise. You will have completed the hero's journey. But this is just the beginning. As Relationship-First Enterprisers, you and your team can look forwards to many other adventures. You'll always be looking for new ways to improve your business. You'll always be looking for new ways to provide more unique value to your customers. And you'll always be looking for new customers. That's the beauty of the Relationship-First Enterprise. There is only growth and opportunity ahead of you. Enjoy.

Epilogue

As the forces of accelerating change, increasing competition, and instant communication sweep across the 21st century marketscape, the world of business will be transformed beyond recognition. To appreciate the impact of these changes, it's helpful to look far into the future and speculate what might happen. So let's look way ahead to the year 2050, and take a peak at three possible tales from the perspective of tomorrow's consumer.

Living Nodes
Nexus Uplands, The Federation of City States
April 9, 2050

Tamarine Star is very pleased. Tao, his nano-sentinel, has forwarded him a bio-message from the Homeowners Syndicate.

"You have qualified for membership in the Homeowners Syndicate. You and your partner Mio can move into your new living node next month. Please make arrangements to change your relationship matrix prior to moving day. Thank you."

Tamarine switches off his multi-dimensional gyro-glasses and summons Tao. "Make arrangements to switch my primary living relationships to the Homeowner Syndicate. Contact apartmentdweller.com and tell them I'm moving out of their unit. We need to cancel my relationship with their insurance company, vapor-net access provider, cleaner, and their moodmodifier-entertainment content network. We are going to be subscribing to the suppliers of the Homeowner Syndicate. Make sure you do everything quickly. I'm really excited about this new relationship."

Looking back a few weeks later, Tamarine realizes he made the right decision. He and Mio were courted by more than 50 different home syndicates. Each offered them a free living node, but only the Homeowners Syndicate was willing to throw in university tuition for their infant boy Malpec. That was the clincher. As well, Homeowners has a great reputation. Tamarine knows dozens of people who have good relationships with them. In fact, the syndicate has the highest relationship-share with homeowners in the world. People love them because they provide thousands of high-quality products and services to homeowners.

When they move into their new living node, Tamarine and Mio won't have to do a thing. Everything will be set up for them. The Syndicate will set up contracts with suppliers for their cold fusion generator, their appliances, furniture, entertainment centre, vapor-net access, and for the luxury sky-buggy in their grav-port. They will also arrange to move their stuff from the apartment. Tamarine is glad he chose to have a relationship with Homeowner Syndicate.

Day Off
August 9, 2050
Upper West Side, New York City

Reclining comfortably in her communications centre, Asper Loc is enjoying her day off. She has the whole day to explore the global experiencefield. Jacking into the Scuba Channel, Asper is greeted by host Will Fondersbrook.

"Welcome back to the Scuba Channel, Asper," Fondersbrook says. "What would you like to do today? Would you like to take a three-dimensional mood-dive on the Coral Reef? Would you like to book a vacation at one of our scuba resorts? Would like to buy a scuba e-book, or perhaps enter one of our real-tone converse-rooms? What's it going to be?"

"I'd like to meet some scuba-divers to talk about night-diving," Asper says. "I also want to get some information about a wreck off the coast of Borneo. Can you search the experiencefield for some meta-media on possible wrecks?"

"Give me 30 seconds, Asper," Fondersbrook says. "Oh yes, here we are. We have a chat taking place on night-diving coming up in 10 minutes. I'll book you in. Do you want to use your own image for the chat, or your usual avatar? As well, I have the search results for that Borneo wreck on your lower-left window right now. These services will cost you $435 inter-credits, plus the warming-tax."

"That's great, Will," Asper says. "I'm very pleased with the service I'm getting from the Scuba Channel. The scuba equipment you sold me last month was excellent. I also enjoyed the e-book you compiled for me last week. Keep up the good work. And if you could, please change the scuba-poster in my kitchen. I would like to see some sharks this evening. My ex-husband is coming over for a chat. I just want to set up the right atmosphere."

Hohoho
Perth, Australia
December 9, 2050

With Christmas Day quickly approaching, Georges Estrada should be in a panic. He needs to buy more than 30 Christmas presents, but he hasn't bought anything yet. Yet Georges isn't worried. He has a relationship with hohoho, the Christmas shopping agents. He has used hohoho for the last five years, and they haven't failed him yet.

"I'm uploading my database list right now," Georges tells Rudolph, the playful little reindeer who hosts the hohoho welcome centre. "I want you to search for the best quality and the lowest prices available out there. I also want you to find me an antique cellular telephone from the turn of the century. My brother Kilgor collects the things."

"Your list is being processed," Rudolph reports. "Yes, things are moving swiftly. Accessing more than 30,000 merchants. Comparing prices.

Finding. Finding. Finding. I've got it. There you go. I've displayed only the good deals. If you put your order through now for all 30 items, we will give you a 10 percent discount, and a free movie from the MovieWatchers. Oh yes, another thing. We have an auction located for the cellular phone. The Antique Lovers Channel is staging it. Will you bid 150 inter-credits?

"Put in the bid," George says. "But don't go any higher than 200."

"You're the buyer at 169," Rudolph reports back seconds later. "I'll add it to Santa's bag. Is there anything else you need right now? Do you need Christmas decorations? A Christmas cake? A non-spliced turkey? Some cards? Don't forget the cards."

"Right, add some Christmas cards to my order Rudolph," Georges says. "And make sure the presents are delivered next Thursday between 1:00 and 3:00 when the kids are at school. Also, wrap the presents. And, oh yeah. Can you have the turkey cooked and delivered to our house at 1 p.m. on Christmas Day?"

"Your order is confirmed," Rudolph says. "Everything will be assembled and wrapped for you. Your turkey will be prepared the way you like it, and delivered at exactly 1:00 p.m. And give us a visit if you need anything else. Have a nice Christmas and a happy new year."

With his Christmas shopping done, Georges wonders what to do next. Should he visit the Golf People for an online clinic, or take a cooking lesson from The Amateur Chef channel? Or maybe he should log into his financial manager. Then again, maybe he should take a nap. After all, Georges is really tired. Christmas shopping really wore him out this year. So much to do, and so little time, George murmurs to himself as he slips into a late afternoon slumber.

Glossary

Attractor Marketing
In today's global economy, prospects are harder to reach. They are less inclined to hear your sales pitch. In order to initiate a relationship with a new customer, you first have to provide free Unique Value in order to "attract" them to your company. This is called Attractor Marketing.

Controlling Promotional Idea
The Controlling Promotional Idea (CPI) is a powerful promotional concept that attracts new prospects to your company. The CPI defines the free Unique Value (UV) you provide prior to a sales pitch or purchase. A CPI is independent of any marketing tool or technology, and can be employed and expanded indefinitely over many years.

Customer Type (CT)
In a Relationship-First Enterprise, all strategic thinking begins with a specific Customer Type (CT). The mission of The Relationship-First Enterprise is to deliver Unique Value to people who match this Customer Type.

Customer Type Specialization
To attract more prospects, The Relationship-First Enterprise can chose Specialized Customer Types such as Female Senior Scuba Divers or Parents With Triplets. By choosing a specialized Customer Type, The Relationship-First Enterprise can create and deliver a higher level of Unique Value by catering to the specific needs of that kind of customer.

Limiting Factors
Limiting Factors are outmoded models, strategies, and systems that stop a company from achieving greater growth. Unlike The Post-Product Realities, which affect a company externally, Limiting Factors are caused by the company itself.

Mass Marketing
In the Industrial Age, most companies served a large homogenous group of customers. The typical Industrial-Age company delivered the same product or service to this mass market, and promoted these using mass marketing tools such as advertising (television, radio, newspapers, magazines, billboards), flyers, direct mail, and PR.

One-To-One Marketing
The exact opposite of Mass Marketing. Companies that employ One-To-One Marketing strategies deliver customized products and services to each individual customer. The One-To-One Marketer uses digital marketing technology to foster a close two-way relationship with customers and prospects. The Relationship-First Enterprise employs One-To-One Marketing strategies to develop Quality Relationships.

Revenue Marketing
When The Relationship-First Enterprise invests a substantial level of time, effort and money to develop high-quality marketing tools and programs, prospects are often willing to pay for them. When this happens, The Relationship-First Enterprise actually makes money from its marketing programs. This is called Revenue Marketing.

Segmented Marketing
In order to focus on the unique needs of individual customers, many companies "segment" or divide their customer base into small groups. Each of these groups is called a Market Segment. The objective is to provide each segment with unique products and services, and promote them through segmented promotional programs.

Style Control Guide
A Style Control Guide establishes the graphic design standards of The

Relationship-First Enterprise. All of the company's communications tools are compiled into this guide to ensure all of the company's logos, fonts, layout elements, and colors are unified.

Technopia
Technopia is a malady that afflicts companies or individuals who become obsessed with the power of technology. Companies with Technopia start their thinking with a specific kind of tool or technology, and build their systems around it. Technopia causes people to lose sight of their real objectives and become mired in complexity.

The Commodity Trap
Companies get caught in The Commodity Trap when they sell a product or service almost identical to their competitor's. Due to instant communication, consumers have the ability to compare the prices of these commodities, which drives down profit margins. Low margins do not give the company enough money to invest in new capabilities or increased Unique Value. Companies that use The Product-First Formula are most likely to become ensnared in The Commodity Trap.

The Definitive Article
A brief document that tells the fundamental story about your company. The Definitive Article is used as the source for all other communications tools: brochures, websites, presentations, advertising, newsletters, and person-to-person communication.

The Event Horizon
Defined as a point in time when an enterprise crosses the threshold into a no-return state of Technopia. Most often, managers are completely unaware their company has crossed The Event Horizon until it is too late and there is no turning back. A common example of this occurs when a company upgrades software; suddenly they find their hardware unable to support the increased internal memory demands, older applications become incompatible and files created by earlier versions unusable.

The Product-First Formula
Stated as Product (P) x Large Number (LN) = Success ($), The Product

First Formula has been used by most companies since the dawn of The Industrial Revolution. Companies that use this formula start all of their strategic thinking with a product, or line of products. This formula has become obsolete due to an accelerating pace of change, intense competition, and instant communication.

The Profit Margin Multiplier

When The Relationship-First Enterprise delivers Unique Value, it no longer suffers from the slim profits found in The Commodity Trap. The company enjoys higher margins because it has no comparable competition. Higher margins give the company more money to invest in developing new forms of Unique Value, which further increases–or multiplies–its profit margins.

The Relationship-First Formula

Stated as Quality Relationships (QR) x Unique Value (UV) equals Success ($), this is the formula for success used by The Relationship-First Enterprise. Companies that use this formula begin all of their strategic thinking with a specific Customer Type (CT), and make it their mission to create and deliver a steadily increasing level of Unique Value to them.

The Technology-First Approach

Companies that take The Technology-First Approach build systems by starting with a particular kind of technology such as a software program. Their company's future growth is constrained by the limitations of the technology, and by the limited vision of the technology developers. In contrast, The Relationship-First Enterprise develops a model system first, and then chooses technology to serve the model.

Value Components

To provide Unique Value (UV) to each customer, The Relationship-First Enterprise divides all of its products and services into their smallest constituent parts. The Relationship-First Enterprise or its customers are then able to assemble the Value Components (VC) into custom solutions. Value Components give the company the ability to quickly seize unforeseen opportunities as they arise.

Acknowledgements

Writing a book is a long, arduous journey. At every turn, there is a demon to be slain, a trial to be won, and a peak to be climbed. To reach the finish line, the writer needs the blessings of the gods, and the patient, willful support of family, friends, and associates. I am no exception. A legion of supporters have cheered me on. To them I give my sincerest thanks. In particular, I want to thank:

- My wife Ginny. She has patiently coddled me while keeping me honest intellectually;
- My kids Douglas and Robin for keeping everything in perspective;
- My sister Diana, for being supportive of everything I do;
- My friends and colleagues involved with The Big Group of Companies—Curtis Verstraete, Corey Kilmartin, Stephen Lindell, Sonia Marques, and Imran Mohammad. Their work with members of *The BIG Idea Adventure* has helped us develop many new concepts, ideas, and strategies that have found their way into this book.

I must also thank my agent Robert Mackwood for getting my books published around the world in many different languages. Without Robert, no one in Russia, China, Japan, India or Romania would have ever learned how to sell more lobsters or avoid the problem with penguins.

I would also like to thank the following clients and associates for their support: Jim Poe, Rick Bauman, Owen Smith, Gregor Binkley, Martha Howard, Beverly Yates, Jim Bean, Jeff Calibaba, Jess Joss. John Brown, Katherine Bain, Mette Keating, Linda Robinson, Michael Wegener, Mitch Silverstein, Tina Tehranchian, Jason Greenlees, Stephanie Czachor, Jay Miller, Kelly Burnett, Janice Waugh, Jim Towle, Jody Silver, Malcolm Silver, Gary White, Scott Ford, John Durbano, Victor Matos, Wayne Baxter, Roch Beaulieau, Robert Young, Monika Pugliesi, Michael Pugliesi, Harold Agla, Bob Gould, Bob Kowaleski, Terry Ortynsky, Jim Gilbert, Jean-Luc Lavergne, Dawn Frail, Kelly Millar, Patrick Carroll, Garth Myers, Rick Borden, Rex Chan, Karla & Preston Diamond, Tim Yurek, Stuart Paris, Paul Reklaitis, Rob Geiger, Larry Trapani, Steven Stramara, Dean D'Camera, Adrian Davis, Doug McPherson, Ricky Lyons, Jon Singer, Al Singer, David Singer, Andy Wimberly, Alex Nicholson, Tom Miller, Marianne Cherney, Byron Woodman, Romy McPherson, Ben Darwin, Gair Maxwell, Mark Cupp, Kathleen Fry, Claudio DiSante, Byron Meier, Tyler Trute, Doug Edwards, Larry Hamilton, Dan Millar, Brian Seim, Raymond Rupert, David Cohen, Stephanie McCullough, Harold Mertin, Greg Barnsdale, Wendy Kellar, and Dora Vell.

I would also like to thank the thousands of readers who have sent me e-mails from around the world explaining how they've used the strategies and concepts in my previous books. I appreciate your kind words and support. I love hearing from you.

THE BIG IDEA ADVENTURE
GET HELP WITH YOUR BIG IDEA

If you would like help with your BIG Idea, we offer a free Starter Session called The BIG Idea Outfitter. During the session you will:

- Clarify your vision for the future of your business.
- Identify your #1 Customer Type, and your Ideal Customer profile.
- Articulate the three fundamental Peak Benefits you provide (from the perspective of your customers).
- Determine new value you can provide to help your customers achieve their Peak Benefit.
- Develop a BIG Idea: something new, better, and different, that will provide

and differentiate you in the marketplace.

- Package this BIG Idea with a brand name and an elevator speech.
- Learn how you can use your BIG Idea to achieve your full potential.

The 90-minute BIG Idea Outfitter Session is provided free-of-charge to qualified candidates. To book your session, call **416.364.8770** or email **bill_bishop@biginc.com**. You can also visit **www.biginc.com**

HOW TO SELL A LOBSTER

HOW TO SELL A LOBSTER: THE UNCONVENTIONAL MONEY-MAKING SECRETS OF A STREETWISE ENTREPRENEUR.

Are you looking for new ways to have fun and make more money? Are you searching for innovative and perhaps unconventional ways to get new ventures started or to create a bigger and better business? If so, *How To Sell A Lobster* is the perfect book for you.

Based on more than three decades of experience, streetwise entrepreneur Bill Bishop takes you on an hilarious and insightful adventure across the often weird but wonderful business landscape. With the help of his trusted mentor Marketing Mike, Bishop offers innovative approaches, special techniques, and proven strategies that will help you business develop big ideas, reach new customers, make a sale, and turn a profit.

Each chapter is a parable about a real-life business problem: learn how Bishop won a walter contest by selling more than 1,400 lobsters; discover how to get a new venture started by overcoming The First-Member Trap; and find out to increase your sales and profit margins by using The Three Boxes marketing game. Bold action and understanding what makes people tick; these are just some of the unconventional money-making secrets Bill Bishop reveals in this book.

To order, go to **www.amazon.ca** or call **416.364.8770**

THE PROBLEM WITH
PENGUINS

DO YOU HAVE THE PENGUIN PROBLEM?

WOULD YOU LIKE TO STAND OUT FROM YOUR COMPETITION? WOULD LIKE TO ATTRACT MORE HIGH-QUALITY CUSTOMERS, AND MAKE A LOT MORE MONEY?

If so, read The Problem With Penguins. Written by Bill Bishop, author of the world-wide best-seller How To Sell A Lobster, this landmark book explains how to stand out in a crowded marketplace by branding and packaging your BIG Idea.

In his trademark fun and unconventional style, Bishop explains:
- Why most companies will never stand out in their marketplace, and how to avoid a similar fate;
- Innovative methods to create a BIG Idea, something new, better, and different, even in the most traditional companies, industries and product/service categories;
- A step-by-step process to brand and package your BIG Idea;
- How to develop BIG promotional ideas to attract more high-quality prospects;
- 21st Century "packaged" marketing techniques to sell your BIG Idea easier, faster, and for more money;
- Strategies to bring your BIG Idea to market faster and easier, while overcoming inertia, procrastination, and negative thinking; plus
- Dozens of real life examples of successful BIG Ideas created by entrepreneurs in many different industries.

If you want to build a great business, stand out from the other penguins in your industry, and learn how to create, brand, and package BIG Ideas, get off your ice flow, and read The Problem With Penguins.

WHO IS BILL BISHOP?

Bill Bishop, one of the world's leading branding and packaging experts, and the creator of The BIG Idea Adventure, believes passionately in the power of BIG Ideas. Since 1987, Bill and his team of coaches have helped thousands of companies solve the problem with penguins by creating new, better, and different BIG Ideas. Bill has written numerous innovative and unconventional business books, including How To Sell A Lobster—now published in 25 countries in 12 languages, and Strategic Marketing For The Digital Age, considered by many to be the pioneering seminal book about e-Marketing. Bill also travels widely delivering BIG Idea speeches and workshops to audiences around the world. To reach Bill, email **bill_bishop@biginc.com**.

STAY CONNECTED WITH BILL
BIG IDEAS TO SELL MORE AND BE HAPPY

BILL BISHOP

CALL ME
If you want to contact me, call my office @ 416.571.8520 or 416.364.8770 X222

MY EMAIL ADDRESS
My email is: bill_bishop@biginc.com

VISIT MY WEBSITE
www.bishopbigideas.com
On my website, you will find free content from my books, audio CDs, speeches, videos, podcasts and blogs.

CATCH ME ON THE TUBE
I am always posting videos to YouTube from my speeches and workshops. Watch for my regular iPhone uploads direct from my workshop locations.

JOIN FACEBOOK GROUP
We have a group on Facebook called Bishop BIG Ideas. If you're on Facebook, join today.

@BISHOPBIGIDEAS
Got the Twitter bug? Follow me on Twitter @BishopBIGIdeas. I'l keep you posted on any BIG Ideas from me and my clients.

BIG IDEA BLOG
Stay motivated and informed by subscribing to my Blog on my website. I will be posting a blog once a week (unless on holidays).

LINK IN TO BIG IDEAS
Join my network at Linkedin. Send an invitation to me and I will connect with you.

BIG IDEA PODCAST
Subscribe to my PodCast and hear monthly (at least) audio advice about how to sell more, a lot more. To subscribe go to www.bishopbigideas.com.

WWW.BISHOPBIGIDEAS.COM

www.ingramcontent.com/pod-product-compliance
Lightning Source LLC
Chambersburg PA
CBHW032017170526
45157CB00002B/733